Collins

Portuguese
phrasebook

Consultant
Tula Teixeira

First published 1993
This edition published 2007
Copyright © HarperCollins Publishers
Reprint 10 9 8 7 6 5 4 3 2 1 0
Typeset by Davidson Pre-Press, Glasgow
Printed in Malaysia by Imago

www.collins.co.uk

ISBN 13 978-0-00-724673-1
ISBN 10 0-00-724673-0

Using your phrasebook

Your *Collins Gem Phrasebook* is designed to help you locate the exact phrase you need, when you need it, whether on holiday or for business. If you want to adapt the phrases, you can easily see where to substitute your own words using the dictionary section, and the clear, full-colour layout gives you direct access to the different topics.

The Gem Phrasebook includes:

- Over 70 topics arranged thematically. Each phrase is accompanied by a simple pronunciation guide which eliminates any problems pronouncing foreign words.

- A Top ten tips section to safeguard against any cultural faux pas, giving essential dos and don'ts for situations involving local customs or etiquette.

- Practical hints to make your stay trouble free, showing you where to go and what to do when dealing with everyday matters such as travel or hotels and offering valuable tourist information.

- Face to face sections so that you understand what is being said to you. These example mini-dialogues give you a good idea of what to expect from a real conversation.

- Common announcements and messages you may hear, ensuring that you never miss the important information you need to know when out and about.

- A clearly laid-out 3000-word dictionary means you will never be stuck for words.

- A basic grammar section which will enable you to build on your phrases.

- A list of public holidays to avoid being caught out by unexpected opening and closing hours, and to make sure you don't miss the celebrations!

It's worth spending time before you embark on your travels just looking through the topics to see what is covered and becoming familiar with what might be said to you.

Whatever the situation, your *Gem Phrasebook* is sure to help!

Contents

Pronouncing Portuguese

● ●

Portuguese is much easier to read than to speak.
However, the pronunciation guide used in this book
gives as accurate a guide as possible to the sounds
of the language. The syllable to be stressed is
printed in **bold**. Note that in conversation words
tend to run together.

Vowels (a, e, i, o, u)

vowel	example	pronunciation	sounds like
a	saco	**sah**-koo	as in father
	fama	**fum**uh	hum
	fica	**fee**kuh	about
e	terra	**terr**-uh	terror
	enorme	eh-**norm**	enquire
	especial	eesh-pess**yahl**	happy
	de	duh	about
i	fica	**fee**kuh	police
	médico	**med**eekoo	happy
o	cobra	**koh**-bruh	all
	homem	**om**ayñ	au pair
	vaso	**vah**-zoo	boot
u	luvas	**loo**vush	boot

7

Notes:
The article **a** sounds like uh (as in the), unless stressed, i.e. **à** (ah).

e can sound like ay, e.g. **fecho** (**fay**shoo), but tends to be silent at the end of words, e.g. **pode** (pod) unless stressed, e.g. **bebé** (be-**be**). The word **e** (meaning and) always sounds like ee.

The article **o** and the letter **o** at the end of words always sound like oo.

Vowel combinations

ai	mais	mysh
ei	peixe	paysh
oi	coisa	**koy**-zuh
ou	outro	**oh**-troo

Nasal vowels

Vowels with a **tilde** ~ or followed by **m** or **n** in the same syllable should be pronounced nasally (letting air out through the nose as well as the mouth), as in French. We have represented this sound in the pronunciation by ñ, e.g.

| **tem** = tayñ | **com** = koñ | **um** = ooñ |
| **pão** = powñ | **manhã** = mun-**yañ** | **põe** = poyñ |

Other letters

ç	**serviço**	ser**vee**_soo_	
ch	**chá**	_shah_	
g	**gelo**	**zhay**-loo	as in mea_s_ure
h			always silent
j	**loja**	**lozh**uh	as in mea_s_ure
lh	**mulher**	mool-**yehr**	
nh	**tenho**	**ten**-yoo	
r/rr	always rolled; 'r' at beginning of word and double 'rr' are forceful and guttural (similar to French 'r')		
s	(between vowels) **coisa** **koy**-_z_uh		
	(after vowel and at end of word) **está** _shta_, **lápis** **lah**-pee_sh_		
x	**caixa** **ky**-_sh_uh		
z	(at end of word) **faz** fa_sh_		

9

Top ten tips

1 Use the formal form of address until you are asked to use the familiar form. Wait until you are invited to use first names.
2 Appearances are important and you should dress according to the occasion.
3 It is a legal requirement in Portugal that everyone carries photographic proof of identity at all times.
4 The Portuguese are very proud of their culture, which is different from that of Spain!
5 To hire a car you often have to be at least 21, depending on the car hire company.
6 The Portuguese have a sweet tooth; try some of their specialities such as **Toucinho do Céu** (heaven's bacon) and **Barriga de Freira** (nun's belly).
7 Most shopping centres are open 7 days a week from 10am to 11pm or in some cases until midnight.
8 There are more than one thousand recipes to cook cod; one of the most famous is **Bacalhau à Brás**.
9 In restaurants, you have to ask for the bill; it's considered impolite of the waiter to bring the bill if you haven't asked for it.
10 Bars and restaurants tend to close on Sundays.

Talking to people

Hello/goodbye, yes/no

You will find the Portuguese are quite ceremonious and will appreciate it if you take the same approach to them as they take towards you.

Please	**Por favor/Faz favor**
	poor fuh-**vor**/fash fuh-**vor**
Thank you	**Obrigado(a)**
	oh-bree**gah**-doo(-duh)
Thanks very much	**Muito obrigado(a)**
	mweento oh-bree**gah**-doo(-duh)
You're welcome!	**De nada!**
	duh **nah**-duh!
Yes	**Sim**
	seeñ
No	**Não**
	nowñ
OK!	**Está bem**
	shta bayñ
Sir/Mr	**Senhor/Sr.**
	sun-**yor**

11

Madam/Mrs/Ms	**Senhora/Sra.**
	sun-**yo**ruh
Miss	**Menina**
	muh-**nee**nuh
Hello/Hi	**Olá**
	oh-**lah**
Goodbye/Bye	**Adeus**
	a**day**-oosh
See you later	**Até logo**
	uh-**te log**oo
See you tomorrow	**Até amanhã**
	uh-**te** amun-**yañ**
Good morning	**Bom dia**
	boñ **dee**-uh
Good afternoon/	**Boa tarde**
evening	**boh**-uh tard
Goodnight	**Boa noite**
	boh-uh noyt
Excuse me!	**Por favor!**
(to catch attention)	poor fuh-**vor**!
Sorry!	**Desculpe!**
	dush**koolp**!
How are you?	**Como está?**
	koh-moo shta?
Fine, thanks	**Bem, obrigado(a)**
	bayñ, oh-bree**gah**-doo(-duh)
And you?	**E você?**
	ee voh-**say**?

I don't understand	**Não compreendo**
	nowñ koñpree-**en**doo
Do you speak English?	**Fala inglês?**
	fah-luh eeñ**glaysh**?

Key phrases

••••••••••••••••••••••••••••••••••

The easiest way to ask for something is by naming what you want and adding **por favor** (poor fuh-**vor**).

the (masculine)	**o/os**
	oo/oosh
glass/glasses	**o copo/os copos**
	oo **kop**oo/oosh **kop**oosh
a/one glass	**um copo**
	ooñ **kop**oo
the (feminine)	**a/as**
	uh/ush
key/keys	**a chave/as chaves**
	uh shahv/ush **shah**-vush
a/one key	**uma chave**
	oomuh shahv
my (masculine)	**o meu**
	oo **may**oo
(feminine)	**a minha**
	uh **meen**-yuh

13

my glass	**o meu copo** oo **may**oo **ko**poo
my key	**a minha chave** uh **meen**-yuh shahv
his/your	**o seu/a sua** oo **say**oo/uh **soo**-uh
his/your glass	**o seu copo** oo **say**oo **kop**oo
his/your key	**a sua chave** uh **soo**-uh shahv
Do you have...?	**Tem...?** tayñ...?
Do you have a room?	**Tem um quarto?** tayñ ooñ **kwar**too?
Do you have any milk?	**Tem leite?** tayñ layt?
Do you have stamps	**Tem selos?** tayñ **sel**oosh?
I'd like...	**Queria...** **kree**-uh...
I'd like an ice cream	**Queria um gelado** **kree**-uh ooñ zhuh-**lah**-doo
I'd like to book a table	**Queria reservar uma mesa** **kree**-uh ruh-zer**var oo**muh **may**-zuh
I'd like pasta	**Queria massa** **kree**-uh **mass**uh
We'd like...	**Queríamos...** **kree**-uhmoosh...

14

We'd like two cakes	**Queríamos dois bolos**
	kree-uhmoosh doysh **boh**loosh
More...	**Mais...**
	mysh...
More bread	**Mais pão**
	mysh powñ
More water	**Mais água**
	mysh **ahg**-wuh
Another...	**Outro(a)**
	oh-troo(truh)
Another milky coffee	**Outro galão**
	oh-troo ga**lowñ**
Another lager	**Outra cerveja**
	oh-truh ser**vay**-zhuh
How much is it?	**Quanto é?**
	kwuñtoo e?
How much does it cost?	**Quanto custa?**
	kwuñtoo **koosh**tuh?
large	**grande**
	gruñd
small	**pequeno**
	puh-**kay**noo
with	**com**
	koñ
without	**sem**
	sayñ
Where is...?	**Onde é...?**
	onduh e...?

Where are...?	**Onde são/estão...?**
	onduh sowñ/shtowñ...?
Where is the toilet?	**Onde é a casa de banho?**
	onduh e uh **kah**-zuh duh **bun**-yoo?
Where are the children?	**Onde estão as crianças?**
	onduh shtowñ ush kree-**un**sush?
How do I get ...?	**Como se vai...?**
	koh-moo suh vy...?
to the station	**para a estação**
	paruh a shtuh-**sowñ**
to the centre	**ao centro**
	ow **sen**troo
There is/are...	**Há...**
	a...
There isn't/ aren't any...	**Não há...**
	nowñ a...
When...?	**Quando...?**
	kwuñdoo...?
At what time...?	**A que hora é...**
	uh kee **or**uh e...
today	**hoje**
	ohzh
tomorrow	**amanhã**
	amun-**yañ**
Can I...?	**Posso...?**
	possoo...?
Can I smoke?	**Posso fumar?**
	possoo foo**mar**?

16

Can I pay?	**Posso pagar?**
	possoo puh-**gar**?
How does this work?	**Como funciona?**
	koh-moo foonss-**yo**nuh?
What does this mean?	**Que quer dizer isto?**
	kuh kayr dee**zehr eesh**too?

Signs and notices

homens	gentlemen
senhoras	ladies
auto-serviço	self-service
aberto	open
fechado	closed
água para beber/ água potável	drinking water
primeiros socorros	first aid
cheio/lotado	full
liquidação total	closing-down sale
caixa	cash desk
empurre	push
puxe	pull
lavabos/sanitários	toilets
livre	vacant/free
ocupado	engaged/occupied
não funciona	out of order

avariado	out of order
para alugar	for hire/rent
para venda	for sale
saldos	sales
cave	basement
rés-do-chão	ground floor
entrada	entrance
bilheteira	ticket office
equitação	horse riding
vagas/vago	vacancies/vacant
banheiro	lifeguard (beach)
casas de banho	bathrooms
degustação	tasting
pagar na caixa	pay at cash desk
depósito de bagagens	left luggage
quente	hot
proibido	forbidden/no...
não mexer/não tocar	do not touch
completo	no vacancies
vestiários	changing rooms
impedido	engaged
descontos	reductions
informações	information
perigo	danger
fumadores	smoking

Polite expressions

●●●●●●●●●●●●●●●●●●●●●●●●●●●●●●●●

There are three forms of address in Portuguese: formal (**o senhor/a senhora**), semi-formal (**você** – for both sexes) and informal (**tu** – for both sexes). Always stick to the formal when addressing older people to whom deference is due, or the semi-formal for people of your own age and status, until you are invited to use the informal **tu**.

The meal was delicious	**A refeição estava deliciosa** uh ruhfay-**sowñ shtah**vuh duhlees-**yoh**zuh
Thank you very much	**Muito obrigado(a)** **mweeñ**too oh-bree**gah**-doo(-duh)
This is a gift for you	**Isto é um presente para si** **eesh**too e ooñ pruh-**zeñt pa**ruh see
Pleased to meet you	**Muito prazer** **mweeñ**too pruh-**zehr**
This is my husband	**Este é o meu marido** esht e oo **may**oo muh**ree**doo
This is my wife	**Esta é a minha mulher** **esh**tuh e uh **meen**-yuh mool-**yehr**
Enjoy your holiday!	**Boas férias!** **boh**-ush **fehr**-yush!

Celebrations

• •

Merry Christmas!	**Bom Natal!**
	boñ nuh-**tahl**!
Happy New Year!	**Feliz Ano Novo!**
	fuh-**leesh ah**-noo **noh**-voo!
Happy birthday!	**Feliz aniversário!**
	fuh-**leesh** aneever-**sar**-yoo!
Have a good trip!	**Muito boa viagem!**
	mweeñtoo **boh**-uh vee-**ah**-zhayñ!

Making friends

• •

In this section we have used the familiar form **tu** for the questions. **Tu** is widely used between young people soon after being introduced, and between close friends and relatives of any age.

FACE TO FACE

A **Como te chamas?**
koh-moo tuh **shah**-mush?
What's your name?

B **Chamo-me...**
shah-moo-muh...
My name is...

A **De onde és?**
duh **oñ**duh esh?
Where are you from?

B **Sou inglês/inglesa**
soh eeñ**glaysh**/eeñ**glay**zuh
I'm English (masc./fem.)

A **Muito prazer**
mweento pruh-**zehr**
Pleased to meet you

How old are you?	**Quantos anos tens?**	
	kwuñtoosh **ah**-noosh tayñsh?	
I'm ... years old	**Tenho ... anos**	
	ten-yoo ... **ah**-noosh	
Where do you live?	**Onde vives?**	
	oñduh **vee**vush?	
Where do you live? (plural)	**Onde vivem?**	
	oñduh vee**vayñ**?	
I live in London	**Vivo em Londres**	
	vee-voo ayñ **loñ**drush	
I'm still studying	**Sou estudante**	
	soh shtoo**duñt**	
I work	**Trabalho**	
	truh-**bahl**-yoo	
I'm retired	**Sou reformado(a)**	
	soh refoor**mah**-doo(uh)	
I'm...	**Sou...**	
	soh...	

21

single	**solteiro(a)**
	sol**tay**-roo(uh)
married	**casado(a)**
	ka**zah**-doo(uh)
divorced	**divorciado(a)**
	deevoors-**yah**-doo(uh)
I have...	**Tenho...**
	ten-yoo...
a boyfriend	**namorado**
	nuh-moo-**rah**-doo
a girlfriend	**namorada**
	nuh-moo-**rah**-duh
a partner	**companheiro(a)**
	koñpun-**yay**-roo(uh)
I have ... children	**Tenho ... filhos**
	ten-yoo ... **feel**-yoosh
I have no children	**Não tenho filhos**
	nowñ **ten**-yoo **feel**-yoosh
I'm here...	**Estou aqui...**
	shtoh uh-**kee**...
on holiday	**de férias**
	duh **fehr**-yush
for work	**por motivo de trabalho**
	poor moo**tee**-voo duh
	truh-**bahl**-yoo

> **Leisure/interests** (p 64) > **Sport** (p 68)

Work

• •

What work do you do?	**Em que trabalha?** ayñ kuh truh-**bahl**-yuh?
I'm...	**Sou...** soh...
a doctor	**médico(a)** **med**eekoo(uh)
a teacher	**professor(a)** proofuh-**sor**(uh)
an engineer	**engenheiro(a)** eñzhun-**yay**-roo(uh)
I work in...	**Trabalho...** truh-**bahl**-yoo ayñ...
a shop	**numa loja** **oo**muh **lozh**uh
a factory	**numa fábrica** **oo**muh **fahb**reekuh
a bank	**num banco** ooñ **buñ**koo
I work from home	**Trabalho em casa** truh-**bahl**-yoo ayñ **kah**-zuh
I'm self-employed	**Trabalho por conta própria** truh-**bahl**-yoo poor **koñ**-tuh **pro**pree-uh
I don't work	**Não trabalho** nowñ truh-**bahl**-yoo

23

Weather

chuveiros/aguaceiros shoo-**vay**roosh/ ugwuh-**say**roosh	showers
limpo **leeñ**poo	clear
a chuva uh **shoo**vuh	rain
nublado noo**blah**-doo	cloudy

It's sunny   **Faz sol**
                    fash sol

It's raining   **Está a chover**
                    shta uh shoo**vehr**

It's windy   **Está vento**
                    shta **veñ**too

What a lovely day! **Que lindo dia!**
                    kuh **leeñ**doo **dee**-uh!

What awful   **Que mau tempo!**
weather!   kuh mow **teñ**poo!

It's very hot/cold **Está muito calor/frio**
                    shta **mweeñ**to ka**lor**/**free**-oo

What is the   **Qual é a temperatura?**
temperature?   kwal e uh teñpra**too**ruh?

Getting around

Asking the way

em frente ayñ freñt	opposite
ao lado de ow **lah**-doo duh	next to
perto de **pehr**too duh	near to
o semáforo	traffic lights
oo suh-**maf**ooroo	
na esquina nuh **shkee**nuh	at the corner

FACE TO FACE

A **Por favor, senhor/senhora! Como se vai à estação?**
poor fuh-**vor**, sun-**yor**/sun-**yor**uh! **koh**-moo suh vy a shtuh-**sowñ**?
Excuse me, sir/madam! How do I/we get to the station?

B **Siga em frente até a igreja e depois vire à esquerda/direita**
see-guh ayñ freñt uh-**te** uh ee-**greh**zhuh ee duh-**poysh vee**ree a eesh-**ker**duh/dee-**ray**tuh
Keep straight on up to the church and then turn left/right

25

A É longe?
e loñzh?
Is it far?

B Não, duzentos metros/cinco minutos
nowñ, doo-**zen**toosh **met**roosh/**seeñ**koo
  mee-**noo**toosh
No, 200 metres/5 minutes

A Obrigado(a)!
oh-bree**gah**-doo(-duh)!
Thanks!

We're lost	**Estamos perdidos** **shtah**-moosh perdee-doosh
Is this the right way to...?	**É este o caminho para...?** e esht oo kuh-**meen**-yoo **pa**ruh...?
Can you show me where it is on the map?	**Pode-me mostrar no mapa?** **pod**-muh moosh-**trar** noo **mah**-puh?

YOU MAY HEAR...

Depois de passar a ponte de**poysh** duh puh-**sar** uh poñt	After passing the bridge
lá lah	Over there
ali/aqui a**lee**/uh-**kee**	there/here

> **Maps and guides** (p 59)

Bus and coach

●●●

FACE TO FACE

A **Por favor, senhor/senhora! Que autocarro vai ao centro da cidade?**

poor fuh-**vor**, sun-**yor**/sun-**yor**uh kuh owtoo-**karr**oo vy ow **señ**troo duh see**dahd**?

Excuse me, sir/madam! Which bus goes to the city centre?

B **Número 15**

noomeroo **keeñ**zuh

Number 15

A **Onde apanho o autocarro?**

oñduh uh-**pahn**-yoo oo owtoo-**karr**oo?

Where do I catch the bus?

B **Ali, em frente da farmácia**

a**lee**, ayñ freñt duh far**mass**-yuh

There, in front of the pharmacy

Is there a bus to...?	**Há autocarro para...?** a owtoo-**karr**oo **pa**ruh...?
to the centre	**para o centro** **pa**ruh oo **señ**troo
to the beach	**para a praia** **pa**ruh uh **pry**-uh

27

How often are the buses to...?	**Que frequência têm os autocarros para...?**
	kuh fruh-**kwayñs**yuh tay-**ayñ** oosh owtoo-**karr**oosh **pa**ruh...?
When is the first/the last bus to...?	**A que horas é o primeiro/ o último autocarro para...?**
	uh kee **or**uz e oo pree**may**-roo/ oo **ool**teemoo owtoo-**karr**oo **pa**ruh...?
Please tell me when to get off	**Pode-me dizer quando devo saír?**
	pod-muh dee**zehr kwuñ**doo **deh**-voo sah-**eer**?
This is my stop	**Esta é a minha paragem**
	esh-tuh e uh **meen**-yuh

YOU MAY HEAR...

Este autocarro não pára em... aysht owtoo-**karr**oo nowñ **pah**-ruh ayñ...	This bus doesn't stop in...
Tem que apanhar o... tayñ kuh apun-**yar** oo...	You must catch the...

Metro

••

You can buy either **uma caderneta de 10 viagens**, which is valid for 10 journeys without time limit, or **um passe**, which covers a month's travel on both bus and metro.

entrada ehñ**trah**-duh	entrance
saída sah-**ee**duh	way out/exit
a linha de metro uh **leen**-yuh duh **met**roo	metro line

Where is the nearest metro station?	**Onde é a estação de metro mais próxima?** **oñ**duh e uh shtuh-**sowñ** duh **met**roo mysh **pross**eemuh?
How does the ticket machine work?	**Como funciona a máquina automática?** **koh**-moo foonss-**yo**nuh uh **mak**eenuh owtoo**mah**-teekuh?
Do you have a map of the metro?	**Tem um mapa do metro?** tayñ ooñ **mah**-puh doo **met**roo?
I'm going to...	**Vou a...** voh uh...
Do I have to change?	**Tenho que mudar?** **ten**-yoo kuh moo**dar**?

Which line is it for...?	**Qual é a linha para...?**
	kwal e uh **leen**-yuh **pa**ruh...?
In which direction?	**Em que direcção?**
	ayñ kuh deereh**sowñ**?
What is the next stop?	**Qual é a próxima paragem?**
	kwal e uh **prosse**emuh puh-**rah**-zhayñ?
Excuse me!	**Com licença!**
	koñ lee-**señ**suh!

Train

....

There are two types of train ticket for all trains:
primeira classe and **segunda classe** (1st and 2nd class). On longer trips, where it is advisable to book ahead (**reservar lugares**), trains may be called **Rápidos** (fast), **Intercidades** or **Alfa** (both modern, fast intercity trains).

a estação	uh shtuh-**sowñ**	station
partidas	par**tee**dush	departures
chegadas	shuh-**gah**-dush	arrivals

Where is the station?	**Onde é a estação?**
	oñduh e uh shtuh-**sowñ**?
First/Second class	**Primeira/Segunda classe**
	pree**may**ruh/se**goon**duh klass

> **Luggage** (p 80)

Smoking/ No smoking	**Fumador/Não fumador**
	foomuh-**dor**/nowñ foomuh-**dor**
I want to book a seat on the Alfa to Aveiro	**Queria reservar um lugar no Alfa para Aveiro**
	kree-uh ruh-zer**var** ooñ loo**gar** noo **ahl**fuh **pa**ruh a**vay**roo
When does it arrive in...?	**A que horas chega a...?**
	uh kee **o**rush **sheh**-guh uh...?
Do I have to change?	**Tenho que mudar?**
	ten-yoo kuh moo**dar**?

FACE TO FACE

A **Quando é o próximo comboio para...?**
kwuñdoo e oo **pross**eemoo koñ**boy**oo **pa**ruh...?
When is the next train to...?

B **Às 17.00**
ash dezuh-**set**uh **o**rush
At 17.00

A **Queria três bilhetes, por favor**
kree-uh traysh beel-**yetsh** poor fuh-**vor**
I'd like three tickets, please

B **Só de ida ou ida e volta?**
soh duh **ee**duh oh **ee**duh ee **vol**tuh?
Single or return?

A **Ida e volta, por favor**
eeduh ee **vol**tuh poor fuh-**vor**
Return, please

Where?	**Onde?**
	oñduh?
Which platform does it leave from?	**De que plataforma parte?**
	duh kuh platuh**for**muh part?
Is this the right platform for the train to...?	**É esta a plataforma do comboio para...?**
	e **esh**tuh uh platuh**for**muh doo koñ**boy**oo **pa**ruh...?
Is this the train for...?	**É este o comboio para...?**
	e aysht oo koñ**boy**oo **pa**ruh...?
Does the train stop at...?	**O comboio pára em...?**
	oo koñ**boy**oo **pah**-ruh ayñ...?
Please let me know when we get to...	**Por favor diga-me quando chegarmos a...?**
	poor fuh-**vor dee**guh-muh **kwuñ**doo shuh-**gar**-mooz uh...?
Is there a buffet on the train?	**Há um vagão restaurante no comboio?**
	a ooñ vuh-**gowñ** rushtoh-**ruñt** noo koñ**boy**oo?
Is this (seat) free?	**Está livre?**
	shta **lee**vruh?
Excuse me	**Perdão/Desculpe**
	per**dowñ**/dush**koolp**

> **Luggage** (p 80)

Taxi

● ●

a praça de taxis uh **prah**-suh duh **tak**seesh	taxi rank

I need a taxi	**Preciso de um táxi** pre-**see**zoo dooñ **tak**see
Where can I/ we get a taxi?	**Onde se pode arranjar um** **táxi?** **oñ**duh suh pod arruñ**zhar** ooñ **tak**see?
Please order me a taxi	**Por favor chame-me um táxi** poor fuh-**vor shah**-muh-muh ooñ **tak**see
How much will it cost by taxi...?	**Quanto custa ir de táxi...?** **kwuñ**too **koosh**tuh eer duh **tak**see...?
to the centre	**ao centro** ow **señ**troo
to the station	**à estação** a shtuh-**sowñ**
to the airport	**ao aeroporto** ow uh-ayroo-**por**too
to this address	**a esta morada** uh **esh**tuh moo**rah**-duh
Please take me to...	**Por favor leve-me a...** poor fuh-**vor lev**-muh uh...

Please take us to...	**Por favor leve-nos a...**
	poor fuh-**vor** lev-noosh uh...
How much is it?	**Quanto é?**
	kwuñtoo e?
Why are you charging me so much?	**Porque está a pedir tanto?**
	poorkuh shta uh ped**eer tuñ**too?
It's more than on the meter	**É mais do que marca no contador**
	e mysh doo kuh **mar**kuh noo koñtuh-**dor**
Keep the change	**Guarde o troco**
	gward oo **tro**koo
Sorry, I don't have any change	**Desculpe, não tenho troco**
	dush**koolp**, nowñ **ten**-yoo **tro**koo
I'm in a hurry	**Tenho muita pressa**
	ten-yoo **mweeñ**tuh **press**uh
Is it far?	**É longe?**
	e loñzh?

Boat and ferry

......

a travessia	crossing
uh truh-**vess**-yuh	
o cruzeiro oo kroo**zay**roo	cruise
o camarote	cabin
oo kumuh-**roht**	

When is the next boat to...?	**Quando parte o próximo barco para...?**
	kwuñdoo part oo **pross**eemoo **bar**koo **pa**ruh...?
Is there a car ferry to...?	**Há um ferry-boat para...?**
	a ooñ ferry-boat **pa**ruh...?
How much is a ticket...?	**Quanto é o bilhete...?**
	kwuñtoo e oo beel-**yet**...?
single/return	**de ida/de ida e volta**
	deeduh/**dee**duh ee **vol**tuh
A tourist ticket	**Um bilhete de segunda classe**
	ooñ beel-**yet** duh se**goon**duh klass
How much is the crossing for a car and ... people?	**Quanto é a passagem para ... pessoas e um carro?**
	kwuñtoo e uh puh-**sah**-zhayñ **pa**ruh ... puh-**so**-ush ee ooñ **kar**roo?
How long is the journey?	**Quanto dura a viagem?**
	kwuñto **doo**ruh vee-**ah**-zhayñ?
What time do we get to...?	**A que horas chegamos a...?**
	uh kee **or**ush shuh-**gah**-moosh uh...?
Where does the boat leave from?	**De onde parte o barco?**
	dee**oñ**duh part oo **bar**koo?
When is...?	**A que horas é...?**
	uh kee **or**uz e...?
the first boat	**o primeiro barco**
	oo pree**may**-roo **bar**koo
the last boat?	**o último barco**
	oo **ool**teemoo **bar**koo

Air travel

How do I get to the airport?	**Como se vai para o aeroporto?** **koh**-moo suh vy **pa**ruh oo ayroo-**por**too?
To the airport, please	**Para o aeroporto, por favor** **pa**ruh oo ayroo-**por**too, poor fuh-**vor**
How long does it take to get to the airport?	**Quanto tempo leva a chegar ao aeroporto?** kwuñtoo **teñ**poo **leh**-vuh uh shuh-**gar** ow uh-ayroo-**por**too?
How much is the taxi fare...?	**Quanto custa ir de táxi...?** **kwuñ**too **koosh**tuh eer duh **tak**see...?
into town	**para o centro** **pa**ruh oo **señ**troo
to the hotel	**para o hotel** pro oh-**tel**
Where do I check in for...(airline)?	**Onde faço o check-in para...?** **oñ**duh **fah**-soo oo check-in **pa**ruh...?
Where is the luggage for the flight from...?	**Onde está a bagagem do voo de...?** **oñ**duh shta uh buh-**gah**-zhayñ doo **voh**-oo duh...?

36

| O seu voo está atrasado oo **sayoo voh**-oo shta atruh-**zah**-doo | Your flight is delayed |

Customs control

••••••••••••••••••••••••••••••••

With the Single European Market, EU citizens are subject only to highly selective spot checks and can go through the blue customs channel (unless they have goods to declare).

| UE   oo ay | EU |
| **bilhete de identidade** beel-**yet** duh eedeñtee**dahd** | identity card |

Do I have to pay duty on this?	**É preciso pagar direitos para isto?** e pre-**see**zoo puh-**gar** deeray-toosh **pa**ruh **eesh**too?
It is for my own personal use	**É para uso pessoal** e **pa**ruh **oo**zoo puh-**swahl**
We are in transit	**Estamos aqui em trânsito** **shtah**-moosh uh-**kee** ayñ **truñ**zeetoo
We are going to...	**Vamos a...** **vuh**-moosh uh...

> **Luggage** (p 80)

37

Driving

Car hire

. . . .

a carta de condução uh **kar**tuh duh koñdoo**sowñ**	driving licence
o seguro oo se**goo**roo	insurance
a marcha atrás uh **mar**shuh uh-**trash**	reverse gear

I'd like to hire a car	**Queria alugar um carro** **kree**-uh aloo**gar** ooñ **karr**oo
for ... days	**para ... dias** **pa**ruh ... **dee**-ush
the weekend	**o fim-de-semana** oo feeñ duh suh-**mah**-nuh
What are your rates...?	**Quais são as tarifas...?** kwysh sowñ ush tuh-**ree**-fush...?
per day/per week	**por dia/por semana** poor **dee**-uh/poor suh-**mah**-nuh
How much is the deposit?	**Quanto deixo de sinal?** **kwuñ**too **day**-shoo duh see**nahl**?
Is there a kilo- metre charge	**Paga-se quilometragem?** **pah**-guh-suh keelome**trah**-zhayñ?

38

Is fully comprehensive insurance included?	**Inclui o seguro contra todos os riscos?** eeñ-**klwee** oo se**goo**roo **koñ**truh **toh**-doosh oosh **reesh**koosh?
Do I have to return the car here?	**Tenho que devolver o carro aqui?** **ten**-yoo kuh duh-vol**vehr** oo **karr**oo uh-**kee**?
By what time?	**A que horas?** uh kuh **or**ush?
I'd like to leave it in...	**Gostaria de o deixar em...** gooshtuh-**ree**-uh duh oo day**shar** ayñ...
What shall I do if the car breaks down?	**Que devo fazer se o carro se avariar?** kuh **deh**-voo fa**zehr** suh oo **karr**oo suh avaree**ar**?
How can I get in touch with you, if needed?	**Como devo entrar em contacto, se necessário?** **koh**-moo **deh**-voo ayn**trar** ayñ koñ**tak**too, suh nussuh-**sar**-yoo?

Car hire

YOU MAY HEAR...

Por favor devolva o carro com o depósito cheio poor fuh-**vor** duh-**vol**vuh oo **karr**oo koñ oo duh-**poz**eetoo **shay**oo	Please return the car with a full tank

39

Driving and petrol

sem chumbo sayñ **shoom**boo	unleaded
gasóleo ga**zol**-yoo	diesel
a gasolina uh gazoo-**lee**nuh	petrol
a bomba de gasolina uh **boñ**buh duh gazoo-**lee**nuh	petrol pump

Can I/we park here? **Pode-se estacionar aqui?**
pod-suh shtass-yoo**nar** uh-**kee**?

How long for? **Por quanto tempo?**
poor **kwuñ**too **teñ**poo?

Do I/we need a parking ticket? **É preciso um bilhete?**
e pre-**see**zoo ooñ beel-**yet**?

Fill it up, please **Encha, por favor**
eñshuh, poor fuh-**vor**

Can you check the oil/the water? **Pode ver o óleo/a água?**
pod vehr oo **ol**-yoo/uh **ahg**-wuh?

...euros worth of unleaded petrol **...euros de gasolina sem chumbo**
...**eur**oosh duh gazoo-**lee**nuh sayñ **shoom**boo

Can you check the tyre pressure, please? **Pode ver a pressão dos pneus, por favor?**
pod vehr uh pruh**sowñ** doosh **pnay**-oosh, poor fuh-**vor**?

40

| Can I pay by credit card? | **Posso pagar com cartão de crédito?** |
| | **poss**oo puh-**gar** koñ kar**towñ** duh **kred**eetoo? |

| **Que bomba usou?** kuh **boñ**buh oo**zoh**? | Which pump did you use? |

Breakdown

Can you help me?	**Pode-me ajudar?**
	pod-muh azhoo**dar**?
My car has broken down	**Tenho o carro avariado**
	ten-yoo oo **karr**oo avaree-**ah**-doo
The car won't start	**O carro não pega**
	oo **karr**oo nowñ **peh**-guh
I've run out of petrol	**Não tenho gasolina**
	nowñ **ten**-yoo gazoo-**lee**nuh
Is there a garage near here?	**Há alguma garagem por aqui?**
	a al**goo**muh ga**rah**-zhayñ poor uh-**kee**?
It's leaking...	**Está a perder...**
	shta uh per**dehr**...
petrol	**gasolina**
	gazoo-**lee**nuh

Breakdown

41

oil	óleo
	ol-yoo
water	água
	ahg-wuh
The ... doesn't work properly	O/A ... não funciona bem
	oo/uh ... nowñ foonss-**yo**nuh bayñ

Car parts

. . . .

The ... doesn't work	O/A ... não funciona
	oo/uh ... nowñ foonss-**yo**nuh
The ... don't work	Os/As ... não funcionam
	oosh/ush ... nowñ foonss-**yo**nowñ

battery	a bateria	batuh-**ree**-uh
bonnet	o capot	kah-**po**
brakes	os travões	tra-**voyñsh**
choke	o motor de arranque	moo**tor** duh a**rruñk**
clutch	a embraiagem	ayñ-bry-**ah**-zhayñ
distributor	o distribuidor	deesh-tree-bwee-**dor**
engine	o motor	moo**tor**
exhaust pipe	o tubo de escape	**too**boo dush**kap**
fuse	o fusível	foo**zee**vel
gears	as mudanças	moo**duñ**sush

handbrake	o travão de mão	tra**vowñ** duh mowñ
headlights	os farois	fa**roysh**
ignition	a ignição	eegnee-**sowñ**
indicator	o indicador	eeñdeekuh-**dor**
points	os platinados	platee-**nah**-doosh
radiator	o radiador	radee-uh-**dor**
rear lights	os pilotos traseiros	pee**lo**toosh tra**zay**roosh
seat belt	o cinto de segurança	**seeñ**too duh segoo**ruñ**-suh
accelerator	o acelerador	asseh
spare wheel	a roda sobres-salente	**rod**uh sobruh-sa**leñt**
spark plugs	as velas	**vel**ush
steering	a direcção	deere**sowñ**
steering wheel	o volante	voo**luñt**
tyre	o pneu	**pnay**-oo
wheel	a roda	**rod**uh
windscreen	o pára-brisas	**pah**-ruh-**bree**zush
washer	o lava pára-brisas	**lah**vuh **pah**-ruh-**bree**zush
wiper	o limpa pára-brisas	**leeñ**puh **pah**-ruh-**bree**zush

Road signs

PERIGO

danger

ALFÂNDEGA

ADUANA

customs

livre

spaces

completo

full

ESTACIONAMENTO
PROIBIDO

no parking

north

Norte

west Oeste

Leste east

Sul

south

diversion

end of roadworks

speed limits are in
kilometres per hour

toll station for
motorway

ÀS
4.ᵃˢ FEIRAS

on Wednesdays

DIAS ÚTEIS
DAS 8 às 20h

weekdays from
8 to 20h

from 6 to 15h

Staying somewhere

Hotel (booking)

● ●

FACE TO FACE

A **Queria reservar um quarto para duas noites**
kree-uh ruh-zer**var** ooñ **kwar**too **pa**ruh **doo**ush **noy**tsh
I'd like to book a room for two nights

B **Individual ou de casal?**
eeñdeeveed-**wahl** oh duh kuh-**zahl**?
Single or double?

A **De casal com uma cama extra para criança,**
por favor
duh kuh-**zahl** koñ **oo**muh **kah**-muh **aysh**-truh **pa**ruh
kree-**uñ**suh, poor fuh-**vor**
Double with an extra bed for a child, please

B **Qual é o preço por noite/por semana?**
kwal e oo **pray**-soo poor noyt/poor suh-**mah**-nuh?
How much is it per night/per week?

from... till...	**do dia... ao dia...**
	doo **dee**-uh... ow **dee**-uh...
with bath	**com casa de banho**
	koñ **kah**-zuh duh **bun**-yoo

with shower	**com chuveiro**
	koñ shoo-**vay**roo
with a double bed	**com cama de casal**
	koñ **kah**-muh duh kuh-**zahl**
twin-bedded	**com duas camas**
	koñ **doo**-ush **kah**-mush
Is breakfast included?	**Inclui o pequeno-almoço?**
	eeñ-**klwee** oo puh-**kay**noo al**moh**-soo?
Can you suggest somewhere else?	**Pode aconselhar outro sítio?**
	pod akoñsel-**yar oh**-troo **seet**yoo?
I'd like to see the room	**Queria ver o quarto**
	kree-uh vehr oo **kwar**too

Hotel (booking)

YOU MAY HEAR...

Não temos vagas nowñ **tay**moosh **vah**-gush	We've no vacancies
Estamos cheios **shtah**-moosh **shay**oosh	We're full up
Para quantas noites? **pa**ruh **kwuñ**tush noytsh?	For how many nights?
O seu nome, por favor? oo **say**oo nom, poor fuh-**vor**?	Your name, please?

Hotel desk

• •

On arrival at a hotel the receptionist will ask for your passport to register your stay. This is an official requirement and must not be misinterpreted.

I booked a room...	**Reservei um quarto...**
	ruh-zer**vay** ooñ **kwar**too...
in the name of...	**em nome de...**
	ayñ nom duh...
Where can I park the car?	**Onde posso estacionar o carro?**
	o**ñ**duh **poss**oo shtass-yoo**nar** oo **karr**oo?
What time is...?	**A que hora é...?**
	uh kee **or**uh e...?
dinner	**o jantar**
	oo zhuñ**tar**
breakfast	**o pequeno-almoço**
	oo puh-**kay**noo al**moh**-soo
The key for room number...	**A chave do quarto número...**
	uh shahv doo **kwar**too **noo**meroo...
I'm leaving tomorrow	**Vou-me embora amanhã**
	voh-muh em**boh**-ruh amun-**yañ**
Please prepare the bill	**Por favor faça a conta**
	poor fuh-**vor fah**-suh **koñ**tuh

48

Camping

....

Have you places?	**Tem vagas?** tayñ **vah**-gush?
We'd like to stay for ... nights	**Gostariamos de ficar ... noites** gooshtuh-**ree**-uhmoosh duh fee**kar** ... noytsh
How much is it per night...?	**Quanto é por noite...?** **kwuñ**too e poor noyt...?
for a tent	**por tenda** poor **teñ**duh
per person	**por pessoa** poor puh-**so**-uh
Are showers...	**Os duches...** oosh **doosh**ush...
Is hot water...	**A água quente...** uh **ahg**-wuh keñt...
Is electricity...	**A electricidade...** uh eeletree-see**dahd**...
...included in the price?	**...são incluidos no preço?** ...sowñ eeñ-**klwee**doosh noo **pray**-soo?
Can we park the caravan/ trailer here?	**Podemos estacionar a caravana/roulotte aqui?** poo**deh**-moosh shtas-yoo**nar** uh karuh-**vah**-nuh/roo**lot** uh-**kee**?

> **Sightseeing and tourist office** (p 62)

Self-catering

●●

If you arrive with no accommodation and want to go self-catering, look for signs saying **Aluguer de Apartamentos** (apartments for rent).

Who do we contact if there are problems?	**Quem podemos contactar em caso de problemas?** kayñ poo**deh**-moosh koñtak**tar** ayñ **kah**-zoo duh proo**bleh**-mush?
How does the heating work?	**Como funciona o aquecimento?** **koh**-moo foon**syo**nuh oo akuh-see**mayñ**too?
Is there always hot water?	**Ha sempre água quente?** a **sayñ**pruh **ahg**-wuh keñt?
Where is the nearest supermarket?	**Onde é o super-mercado mais perto?** **oñ**duh e oo sooper-mer**kah**-doo mysh **pehr**too?

> **Sightseeing and tourist office** (p 62)

Shopping

Shopping phrases

Many shops still close for lunch between 1 and 3 pm, but most now remain open throughout the day. Large department stores and food shops generally stay open from 9 am to 7 pm.

FACE TO FACE

A **Que deseja?**
kuh de**zay**zhuh?
Can I help you?

B **Um/uma..., por favor**
ooñ/**oo**muh ..., poor fuh-**vor**
A ..., please

A **Mais alguma coisa?**
mysh al**goo**muh **koy**-zuh?
Would you like anything else?

B **Não, é tudo. Quanto é?**
nowñ, e **too**doo. **kwuñ**too e?
No, that's all. How much is it?

51

Where is...?	**Onde é...?**	
	oñduh e...?	
Do you have...?	**Tem...?**	
	tayñ...?	
Where can I buy...?	**Onde posso comprar...?**	
	oñduh **posso**o koñ**prar**...?	
toys/gifts	**brinquedos/brindes**	
	breeñ**kay**-doosh/**breeñ**-dush	
It's too expensive for me	**É muito caro para mim**	
	e **mweeñ**too **kah**-roo **pa**ruh meeñ	

Shops

....

saldo/descontos **sahl**doo/dush**koñ**toosh	sale/reductions
liquidação leekeeduh-**sowñ**	closing-down sale
hoje, aberto até às... ohzh, uh-**behr**too uh-**te** ush...	open today until...

baker's	**padaria**	puduh-**ree**-uh
bookshop	**livraria**	leevruh-**ree**-uh
butcher's	**talho**	**tahl**-yoo
cake shop	**pastelaria**	pushtuh-la**ree**-uh
clothes (women's)	**roupa de senhora**	**roh**-puh duh sun-**yor**uh
clothes (men's)	**roupa para homem**	**roh**-puh **pa**ruh **om**ayñ

52

gifts	**brindes**	**breeñ**-dush
glasses	**óculos**	**oh**-kooloosh
greengrocer's	**frutaria**	frootuh-**ree**-uh
grocer's	**mercearia**	mersee-uh-**ree**-uh
hairdresser's	**cabeleireiro(a)**	kuh-buh-lay-**ray**-roo(-ruh)
jeweller's	**joalharia**	zhwal-yuh-**ree**-uh
market	**mercado**	mer**kah**-doo
optician	**oculista**	okoo**leesh**-tuh
pharmacy	**farmácia**	far**mass**-yuh
self-service	**auto-serviço**	ow**too**-ser**vee**soo
shoe shop	**sapataria**	sapuh-tuh-**ree**-uh
shop	**loja**	**lozh**uh
stationer's	**papelaria**	papuh-la**ree**-uh
supermarket	**super-mercado**	sooper-mer**kah**-doo
tobacconist's	**tabacaria**	tabakuh-**ree**-uh
toy shop	**loja de brinquedos**	**lozh**uh duh breeñ**kay**-doosh

Food (general)

•••••••••••••••••••••••••••••••••••

beef	**a carne de vaca**	karn duh **vah**-kuh
biscuits	**as bolachas**	bool**ah**-shush
bread	**o pão**	powñ
bread (brown)	**o pão integral**	powñ eeñtuh-**grahl**
bread roll	**o papo-seco**	**pah**-poo-**seh**-koo
butter	**a manteiga**	muñ**tay**-guh

53

cakes	os bolos	**boh**-loosh
cheese	o queijo	**kay**-zhoo
chicken	a galinha	ga**leen**-yuh
coffee	o café	kuh-**fe**
cream	a nata	**nah**-tuh
crisps	as batatas fritas	bu**tah**-tush **free**tush
eggs	os ovos	**oh**-voosh
fish	o peixe	paysh
flour	a farinha	fa**reen**-yuh
ham (cooked)	o fiambre	fee-**uñ**-bruh
ham (cured)	o presunto	pruh-**zoon**too
honey	o mel	mel
jam	a compota	koñ**pot**uh
lamb	o carneiro	kar**nay**-roo
margarine	a margarina	marguh-**ree**nuh
marmalade	a doce de laranja	dohss duh la**ruñ**zhuh
milk	o leite	layt
olive oil	o azeite	a**zayt**
orange juice	o sumo de laranja	**soo**moo duh la**ruñ**zhuh
pasta	as massas	**mass**ush
pepper	a pimenta	pee**meñ**tuh
pork	a carne de porco	karn duh **por**koo
rice	o arroz	a**rrosh**
salt	o sal	sal

54

stock cube	o cubo	**koo**boo
	concentrado	koñ-sayn**trah**-doo
sugar	o açúcar	uh-**soo**kar
tea	o chá	shah
vinegar	o vinagre	vee**nah**-gruh

Food (fruit and veg)

Fruit

apples	as maçãs	muh-**suñsh**
apricots	os damascos	muh-**mash**koosh
bananas	as bananas	buh-**nah**-nush
cherries	as cerejas	suh-**ray**-zhush
grapefruit	a toranja	too**ruñ**zhuh
grapes	as uvas	**oo**vush
lemon	o limão	lee**mowñ**
melon	o melão	me**lowñ**
nectarines	as nectarinas	nek-tuh-**ree**nush
oranges	as laranjas	la**ruñ**zhush
peaches	os pêssegos	**pay**-suh-goosh
pears	as pêras	**pay**-rush
pineapple	o ananás	anuh-**nash**
plums	as ameixas	a**may**-shush
raspberries	as framboesas	frum-**bway**-zush
strawberries	os morangos	moo**ruñ**goosh
watermelon	a melancia	meluñ-**see**-uh

Vegetables

asparagus	os espargos	**shpar**goosh
aubergine	a beringela	bereeñ-**zhe**luh
cabbage	a couve	kohv
carrots	as cenouras	suh-**noh**-rush
cauliflower	a couve-flor	kohv-**flor**
courgettes	as courgettes	koor**zhetsh**
french beans	o feijão verde	fay-**zhowñ** vehrd
garlic	o alho	**ahl**-yoo
leeks	os alhos-porros	al-yoosh-**porr**osh
lettuce	a alface	al**fass**
mushrooms	os cogumelos	koogoo-**mel**oosh
onions	as cebolas	suh-**bol**ush
peas	as ervilhas	ehr**veel**-yush
peppers	os pimentos	pee**meñ**toosh
potatoes	as batatas	bu**tah**-tush
spinach	os espinafres	shpee**naf**rush
tomatoes	os tomates	too**mahtsh**
turnips	os nabos	**nah**-boosh

Clothes

Size for clothes is **a medida** – shoes is **o número**.

May I try this on? **Posso provar isto?**
possoo proo**var eesh**too?

> **Paying** (p 79)

Where are the changing rooms?	**Onde é o gabinete de provas?**
	oñduh e oo gabee**net** duh **prov**ush?
Have you a size...?	**Tem uma medida...?**
	tayñ **oo**muh muh**dee**-duh...?
bigger/smaller	**maior/mais pequena**
	may**or**/mysh puh-**kay**nuh
Have you this...?	**Tem isto...?**
	tayñ **eesh**too...?
in my size	**na minha medida**
	nuh **meen**-yuh muh**dee**-duh
in other colours	**em outras cores**
	ayñ **oh**-trush **ko**rush
It's too...	**É muito...**
	e **mweeñ**too...
short/long	**curto/comprido**
	koortoo/koñ**pree**doo
I'm just looking	**Só estou a ver**
	so shtoh uh vehr
I'll take it	**Quero comprar**
	kehroo koñ**prar**

women's sizes		men's suit sizes		shoe sizes			
UK	EU	UK	EU	UK	EU	UK	EU
8	36	36	46	2	35	7	41
10	38	38	48	3	36	8	42
12	40	40	50	4	37	9	43
14	42	42	52	5	38	10	44
16	44	44	54	6	39	11	45
18	46	46	56				

De que medida? duh kuh muh**dee**-duh?	What size?
Quer provar? kehr proo**var**?	Do you want to try it on?
Fica bem? **fee**kuh bayñ?	Does it fit?

Clothes (articles)

belt	o cinto	**seeñ**too
blouse	a blusa	**bloo**zuh
bra	o soutien	soot-**yañ**
coat	o casaco	ka**zah**-koo
dress	o vestido	vush**tee**doo
hat	o chapéu	sha**pay**-oo
hat (woollen)	a boina	**boy**nuh
jacket	o casaco curto	ka**zah**-koo **koor**too
knickers	as cuecas	**kwe**kush
nightdress	a camisa de dormir	kuh-**mee**zuh duh door**meer**
pyjamas	o pijama	pee**zhah**-muh
sandals	as sandálias	suñ**dahl**-yush
scarf (wool)	o cachecol	kashu-**kol**
shirt	a camisa	kuh-**mee**zuh
shorts	os calções	kal**soyñsh**
skirt	a saia	**sy**-uh

slippers	as chinelas	shee**nel**ush
socks	as peúgas	**pew**-gush
suit	o fato	**fah**-too
swimsuit	o fato de banho	**fah**-too duh **bun**-yoo
tie	a gravata	gruh-**vah**-tuh
tights	os collants	ko**lañsh**
tracksuit	o fato de treino	**fah**-too duh **tray**-noo
trousers	as calças	**kahl**sush
t-shirt	a camisola	kuhmee**zoh**-luh
underpants	as cuecas	**kwe**kush

Maps and guides

Have you...?	**Tem...?**
	tayñ...?
a map of	**um mapa de...**
(name town)	ooñ **mah**-puh duh...
of the region	**da região**
	duh ruzh-**yowñ**
Can you show	**Pode-me mostrar onde fica ...**
me where ... is	**no mapa?**
on the map?	**pod**-muh moosh-**trar oñ**duh
	feekuh ... noo **mah**-puh?
Do you have a	**Tem um mapa detalhado da**
detailed map	**área?**
of the area?	tayñ ooñ **mah**-puh
	duhtal-**yah**-doo duh **ah**ree-uh?

59

Have you...?	**Tem...?**
	tayñ...?
a guide book	**algum guia**
	al**gooñ ghee**-uh
a leaflet	**algum folheto**
	al**gooñ** fool-**yet**oo
in English?	**em inglês?**
	ayñ eeñ**glaysh**?
Where can I/	**Onde se pode comprar**
we buy English	**jornais ingleses/livros?**
newspapers/	**oñ**duh suh pod koñ**prar**
books?	zhoor**nysh** eeñ**glez**eesh/
	leevroosh?

Post office

. . . .

Main post offices are open from 9 am to 5 pm,
Monday to Friday, and until 1 pm on Saturdays.
Check times in small towns.

os correios	post office
oosh koo**rray**oosh	
o marco do correio	postbox
oo **mar**koo doo koo**rray**oo	
os selos oosh **sel**oosh	stamps

> **Asking the way** (p 25)
> **Sightseeing and tourist office** (p 62)

Is there a post office near here?	**Há algum correio aqui perto?** a al**gooñ** koo**rray**oo uh-**kee pehr**too?
I'd like stamps for … postcards to Great Britain	**Queria selos para … postais para a Grã-Bretanha** **kree**-uh **sel**oosh **pa**ruh … poosh-**tysh** prah grañ-bruh-**tun**-yuh
I want to send this letter registered post	**Queria mandar esta carta registada** **kree**-uh muñ**dar esh**tuh **kar**tuh ruzheesh-**tah**-duh
How much is it to send this parcel?	**Quanto custa mandar este embrulho?** **kwuñ**too **koosh**tuh muñ**dar** aysht aym-**brool**-yoo?
by air	**por avião** poor av-**yowñ**
first class	**por correio azul** poor koo**rray**oo a**zool**

YOU MAY HEAR…

Preencha este impresso pree-**eñ**shuh aysht eeñ**press**oo	Fill in this form

Leisure

Sightseeing and tourist office

••••••••••••••••••••••••••••••••••

The tourist office is called **Turismo**. If you are looking for somewhere to stay, they should have details of hotels, campsites, etc.

Where is the tourist office?
: **Onde é o turismo?**
  oñduh e oo too**reezh**-moo?

We'd like to go to...
: **Gostaríamos de ir a...**
  gooshtuh-**ree**-uhmoosh duh eer uh...

Have you any leaflets?
: **Tem alguns folhetos?**
  tayñ al**goonsh** fool-**yet**oosh?

Are there any excursions?
: **Há algumas excursões?**
  a al**goo**mush shkoor-**soyñsh**?

How much does it cost to get in?
: **Quanto custa a entrada?**
  kwuñtoo **koosh**tuh uh ayn**trah**-duh?

Are there any reductions for...?
: **Fazem descontos para...?**
  fa**zayñ** dush**koñ**toosh **pa**ruh...?

children	**crianças**	
	kree-**uñ**sush	
students	**estudantes**	
	shtoo**duñtsh**	
unemployed	**desempregados**	
	duh-zaympruh-**gah**-doosh	
senior citizens	**terceira idade**	
	ter**say**ruh ee**dahd**	

Entertainment

....

What is there to do in the evenings?	**Que se pode fazer à noite?**
	kuh suh pod fa**zehr** a noyt?
Where do local people go at night?	**Onde a gente de aqui vai à noite?**
	oñduh uh zheñt duh**kee** vy a noyt?
Is there anything for children?	**Há alguma coisa para crianças?**
	a al**goo**muh **koy**-zuh **pa**ruh kree-**uñ**sush?

Leisure/interests

Where can I/ we go...?	**Onde se pode...?**
	oñduh suh pod...?
fishing	**pescar**
	push**kar**
walking	**andar**
	uñ**dar**
Are there any good beaches near here?	**Há algumas praias boas aqui perto?**
	a al**goo**mush **pry**-ush **boh**-ush uh-**kee pehr**too?
Is there a swimming pool?	**Há piscina?**
	a peesh-**see**nuh?

Music

Are there any good concerts on?	**Há algum bom concerto por aqui?**
	a al**goom** boñ koñ**sehr**-too poor uh-**kee**?
Where can one get tickets?	**Onde se compram os bilhetes?**
	oñduh suh koñ**prowñ** oosh beel-**yetsh**?

Where can we hear some fado/folklore?	Onde podemos ouvir o fado/folclore?
	oñduh poo**deh**-moosh oh-**veer** oo **fah**-doo/folk**lo**ruh?

Cinema

• •

In Portugal it is customary to show films in their original versions, with sub-titles.

o cinema	oo see**nay**-muh	cinema
a sessão	uh suh**sowñ**	performance, showing

What's on at the cinema?	Qual é o programa no cinema?
	kwal e oo proo**gruh**-muh noo see**nay**-muh?
When does (name film) start?	A que horas começa ...?
	uh kee **or**ush koo**mess**uh...?
How much are the tickets?	Quanto custam os bilhetes?
	kwuñtoo koosh**towñ** oosh beel-**yetsh**?
Two for the (time) showing	Dois para a sessão das...
	doysh pra suh**sowñ** dush...

Para a sala um/dois não temos lugares paruh uh **sah**-luh ooñ/ doysh nowñ **teh**-moosh loo**gar**ush	For screen 1/2 we have no tickets left

Theatre/opera

· ·

Theatre and opera performances generally start quite late, around 9.30 pm, and finish around midnight.

What's on at the theatre?	**Qual é o programa de teatro?** kwal e oo proo**gruh**-muh duh tee-**ah**-troo
What prices are the tickets?	**Quais são os preços dos bilhetes?** kwysh sowñ oosh **pray**-soosh doosh beel-**yetsh**?
I'd like two tickets...	**Queria dois bilhetes... kree**-uh doysh beel-**yetsh**...
for tonight	**para esta noite pa**ruh **esh**tuh noyt
for tomorrow night	**para amanhã à noite pa**ruh amun-**yañ** a noyt

Leisure

for 5th August	para cinco de Agosto
	paruh **seeñ**koo da**gosh**too
in the stalls	na plateia
	nuh pla**tay**-uh
in the circle	no balcão
	noo bal**kowñ**
in the upper circle	no segundo balcão
	noo se**goon**doo bal**kowñ**
When does the performance begin/end?	Quando começa/acaba o espectáculo?
	kwuñdoo koo**mess**uh/ a**kah**-buh oo shpeh-**tak**ooloo?

Television

....

o telecomando oo tuh-leh-koo**muñ**doo	remote control
ligar lee**gar**	to switch on
desligar dush-lee**gar**	to switch off
o programa oo proo**gruh**-muh	programme
os desenhos animados oosh duh**zayn**-yoosh anee**mah**-doosh	cartoons

Where is the television?	**Onde está o televisor?**
	oñduh shta oo tuh-luh-vee**zor**?
How do you switch it on?	**Como se liga?**
	koh-moo suh **lee**guh?
Which button do I press?	**Que botão uso?**
	kuh boo**towñ oo**zoo?
Please could you lower the volume?	**Por favor pode reduzir o volume?**
	poor fuh-**vor** pod ruhdoo**zeer** oo voo-**loo**-muh?
May I turn the volume up?	**Posso aumentar o volume?**
	possoo owmeñ**tar** oo voo-**loo**-muh?
When is the news?	**Quando são as notícias?**
	kwuñdoo sowñ ush noo-**teess**-yush?
Do you have any English-speaking channels?	**Há alguns canais em inglês?**
	a al**goonsh** kuh-**nysh** ayñ eeñ**glaysh**?

Sport

o campo	oo **kum**poo	pitch/court
empatar	eñpuh**tar**	to draw a match
ganhar	gun-**yar**	to win

Where can I/we...?	Onde se pode...?
	oñduh suh pod...?
play tennis	jogar ténis
	zhoo**gar ten**eesh
play golf	jogar golfe
	zhoo**gar** golf
go swimming	nadar
	nuh-**dar**
see some football	ver futebol
	vehr foot**bol**
How much is it per hour?	Quanto é por hora?
	kwuñtoo e poor **or**uh?
Do you have to be a member?	É preciso ser sócio?
	e pre-**see**zoo sehr **soss**-yoo?
Do they hire out...?	Alugam ...?
	aloo**gowñ**...?
rackets	raquetes
	ra**ket**ush
golf clubs	tacos de golfe
	tah-koosh duh golf
We'd like to go to see (name team) play	Queríamos assistir ao jogo de...
	kreeuh-moosh aseesh**teer** ow **shoh**-goo duh...
Where can we get tickets?	Onde podemos comprar bilhetes?
	oñduh poo**deh**-moosh koñ**prar** beel-**yetsh**?

Outdoor pursuits

Portugal is renowned for its many world-class golf courses, which are a big attraction for visitors, but there are many other leisure activities to choose from. Licences for river fishing can be obtained from local town halls.

Where is the nearest golf course?	**Onde é o campo de golfe mais próximo?** **oñ**duh e oo **kum**poo duh golf mysh **pross**eemoo?
What is your handicap?	**Qual é o seu handicap?** kwal e oo **say**-oo handicap?
My handicap is...	**O meu handicap é...** oo **may**oo handicap e...
Where can we go horse-riding?	**Onde podemos andar a cavalo?** **oñ**duh poo**deh**-moosh uñ**dar** uh ka**vah**-loo?
How much is it...?	**Quanto custa...?** **kwuñ**too **koosh**tuh...?
per hour/per day	**por hora/por dia** por **or**uh/por **dee**-uh
Where's the best place to go fishing?	**Qual é o melhor lugar para ir pescar?** kwal e oo mel-**yor** loo**gar** paruh eer pesh**kar**?

Leisure

> **Maps and guides** (p 59)

| A fishing licence, please | **Uma licença de pesca, por favor** |
| | **oo**muh lee**sayñ**suh duh **pesh**-kuh, poor fuh-**vor** |

Walking

• •

Are there any guided walks?	**Há alguns passeios guiados?**
	a al**goonsh** pa**ssay**oosh ghee-**ah**-doosh?
Do you have details?	**Pode-me dar informações?**
	pod-muh dar eeñfoormuh-**soyñsh**?
Do you have a guide to local walks?	**Tem algum guia dos passeios locais a pé?**
	tayñ al**gooñ ghee**-uh doosh pa**ssay**oosh loo**kysh** uh pe?
How many kilometres is the walk?	**De quantos quilómetros é o passeio?**
	duh **kwuñ**toosh kee**lom**etroosh e oo pa**ssay**oo?
How long will it take?	**Que tempo demora?**
	kuh teñ**poo** duh-**mor**uh?
Is it very steep?	**Tem muitas subidas?**
	tayñ **mweeñ**tush soo**bee**-dush?

Communications

Telephone and mobile

The international code for Portugal is **oo 351** plus the Portuguese number. For calls within Portugal you must use the full area code, even for local calls.

o cartão telefónico oo kar**towñ** tuh-luh-**fo**neekoo	phonecard
a lista telefónica uh **leesh**tuh tuh-luh-**fo**neekuh	phone directory
as páginas amarelas ush **pazh**eenush amuh-**reh**lush	yellow pages
atender uhteñ**der**	to pick up
desligar dushlee**gar**	to hang up

I want to make a phone call

Quero fazer uma chamada telefónica
kehroo fa**zehr oo**muh shuh-**mah**-duh tuh-luh-**fo**neekuh

A Estou/Alô/Sim?
shtoh/a**loh**/seeñ?
Hello?

B Posso falar com...?
possoo fa**lar** koñ...?
Can I speak to...?

A Quem fala?
kayñ **fah**-luh?
Who is speaking?

B Daqui é o Jim Brown
duh-**kee** e oo jim brown
This is Jim Brown

A Um momento
ooñ mo**meñ**-too
Just a moment

Where can I buy a phonecard?	Onde posso comprar um cartão telefónico? **oñ**duh **poss**oo koñ**prar** ooñ kar**towñ** tuh-luh-**fo**neekoo?
Do you have a mobile?	Tem telemóvel? tayñ tuh-luh-**mo**vel?
What is the number of your mobile?	Qual é o número do seu telemóvel? kwal e oo **noo**meroo doo **say**oo tuh-luh-**mo**vel?
My mobile number is...	O meu número de telemóvel é... oo mayoo **noo**meroo duh tuh-luh-**mo**vel e...

73

I would like to speak to...	**Queria falar com...**
	kree-uh fa**lar** koñ...
Senhor Lopes, please	**O Sr. Lopes, por favor**
	oo sun-**yor** lopsh, poor fuh-**vor**
Extension... (number)	**Extensão...**
	shteñ**sowñ**...
I will call back later	**Chamo mais tarde**
	shah-moo mysh tard
I will call back tomorrow	**Chamo amanhã**
	shah-moo amun-**yañ**
I can't get through	**Não consigo ligar**
	nowñ koñ**see**goo lee**gar**

YOU MAY HEAR...

Não desligue nowñ duzh-**leeg**	Hold on
Está impedido shta eeñpuh-**dee**doo	It's engaged
Pode chamar mais tarde? pod shuh-**mar** mysh tard?	Can you try again later?
Quer deixar um recado? kehr day**shar** ooñ re**kah**-doo?	Do you want to leave a message?
É engano e ayn-**guh**-noo	You've made a mistake
É favor desligar o telemóvel e fuh-**vor** dushlee**gar** oo tuh-luh-**mo**vel	Please turn off mobiles

74

Este é o gravador de chamadas de... aysht e oo gravuh-**dor** duh shuh-**mah**-dush duh...	This is the answering machine of...

E-mail

....

The Portuguese for e-mail is **correio electrónico** (koo**rray**oo ele**troh**-neekoo) although most people use the word **e-mail**.

Tem e-mail?	**Tem e-mail?** tayñ e-mayl?
What is your e-mail address?	**Qual é o seu endereço de e-mail?** kwal e oo **say**oo eñ-duh-**re**soo duh e-mayl?
How do you spell it?	**Como se soletra?** **koh**-moo suh soo**let**ruh?
All one word	**Tudo uma palavra** **too**-doo **oo**muh puh**lah**-vruh
All lower case	**Tudo em letras minúsculas** **too**-doo ayñ **let**rush mee**noosh**koolush
My e-mail address is...	**O meu endereço electrónico é...** oo **may**oo eñ-duh-**re**soo ele**troh**-neekoo e...

75

clare.smith@
collins.co.uk

clare.smith@collins.co.uk
clare **poon**too smith arr**oh**-buh
collins **poon**too co **poon**too uk

Internet

....

página principal **pah**-zheenuh preensee**pahl**	home
nome de usuário nom doo ooz**war**yoo	username
navegar nave**gar**	to browse
pesquisador peshkeezuh-**dor**	search engine
senha **sen**-yuh	password
contacte-nos koñ**takt**-noosh	contact us
voltar ao menu vol**tar** ow me**noo**	back to menu
mapa do local **mah**-puh doo loo**kahl**	sitemap

Are there any internet cafés here?
Há alguns cibercafé aqui?
a al**goonsh** seeberkuh-**fe** uh-**kee**?

How much is it to log on for an hour?
Quanto custa ligar à internet por uma hora?
kwuñtoo **koosh**tuh lee**gar** ah eenter**net** poor **oo**muh **or**uh?

Fax

• •

To fax Portugal from the UK, the code is **oo 351**
followed by the Portuguese fax number you require.

Addressing a fax

de	from
à atenção de	for the attention of
data	date
ref.	re:
este documento contem ...	this document contains...
páginas, incluindo esta	pages including this

Do you have a fax?	**Tem fax?**
	tayñ faks?
I would like to send a fax	**Queria mandar um fax**
	kree-uh muñdar ooñ faks
What is your fax number?	**Qual é o seu número de fax?**
	kwal e oo **say**oo **noo**meroo duh faks?
My fax number is...	**O meu número de fax é...**
	oo **may**oo **noo**meroo duh faks e...
Can I send a fax from here?	**Posso mandar um fax daqui?**
	possoo muñdar ooñ faks duh**kee**?

Practicalities

Money

Banks are generally open from 8.30 am to 3 pm, Monday to Friday.

Where is the bank?	Onde é o banco? **oñ**duh e oo **buñ**koo?
Is there a cash dispenser near here?	Há uma caixa automática aqui perto? a **oo**muh **ky**-shuh owtoo**mat**eekuh uh-**kee pehr**too?
Where can I/we change some money?	Onde se pode trocar dinheiro? **oñ**duh suh pod troo**kar** deen-**yay**-roo?
I want to change these traveller's cheques	Quero trocar estes cheques de viagem **kehr**oo troo**kar esh**tush sheksh duh vee-**ah**-zhayñ
When does the bank open/close?	Quando abre/fecha o banco? **kwuñ**doo **ah**-bruh/**fay**shuh oo **buñ**koo?

78

Can I pay with pounds/euros?	Posso pagar em libras/euros?
	possoo puh-**gar** ayñ **lee**brush/ **eoo**-rosh?
Can I use my card with this cash dispenser?	Posso usar o meu cartão nesta caixa?
	possoo oo**zar** oo **may**oo kar**towñ nesh**tuh **ky**-shuh?

Paying

. . . .

a conta	uh **koñ**tuh	bill
a caixa	uh **ky**-shuh	cash desk
a factura	uh fak**too**ruh	invoice
pague na caixa **pah**-guh nuh **ky**-shuh		pay at the cash desk
o recibo	oo ruh-**see**boo	receipt

How much is it?	Quanto é?
	kwuñtoo e?
Can I pay...?	Posso pagar...?
	possoo puh-**gar**...?
by credit card	com cartão de crédito
	koñ kar**towñ** duh **kred**eetoo
by cheque	por cheque
	poor shek
Do you take credit cards?	Aceita cartões de crédito?
	a**say**tuh kar**toyñsh** duh **kred**eetoo?

Is service included?	**O serviço está incluído?** oo ser**vee**soo shta eeñ-**klwee**doo?
Is VAT included?	**O IVA está incluído?** oo ee**vuh** shta eeñ-**klwee**doo?
Put it on my bill	**Ponha na minha conta** **pon**-yuh nuh **meen**-yuh **koñ**tuh
Please can I have a receipt	**Pode-me dar um recibo por favor** **pod**-muh dar ooñ ruh-**see**boo poor fuh-**vor**
Do I pay in advance?	**Paga-se adiantado?** **pah**-guh-suh adyuñ-**tah**-doo?
Where do I pay?	**Onde se paga?** **oñ**duh suh **pah**-guh?
I've nothing smaller	**Não tenho troco** nowñ **ten**-yoo **tro**koo

Luggage

a conta uh **koñ**tuh	bill
a recolha de bagagem uh re**kol**-yuh duh buh-**gah**-zhayñ	baggage reclaim
o carrinho oo ka**rreen**-yoo	trolley

> **Shopping phrases** (p 51)

My luggage hasn't arrived	A minha bagagem não chegou
	uh **meen**-yuh buh-**gah**-zhayñ nowñ shuh-**goh**
My suitcase has arrived damaged	A minha mala chegou danificada
	uh **meen**-yuh **mah**-luh shuh-**goh** duhneefee-**kah**-duh

Repairs

. . . .

sapateiro sapuh-**tay**roo	shoe repair shop
reparações rápidas reparuh-**soyñsh rah**-peedush	repairs while you wait

This is broken	Isto está partido
	eeshtoo shta par**tee**doo
Where can I get this repaired?	Onde posso arranjar isto?
	oñduh **poss**oo arruñ**zhar eesh**too?
Can you repair...?	Pode-me arranjar...?
	pod-muh arruñ**zhar**...?
these shoes	estes sapatos
	ayshtush suh-**pah**-toosh
my watch	o relógio
	oo ruh-**lozh**-yoo

> **Train** (p 30) > **Air travel** (p 36)

How much will it be?	**Quanto vai custar?**
	kwuñtoo vy koosh**tar**?
Can you do it straightaway?	**Pode fazer imediatamente?**
	pod fa**zehr** eemuh-dee-ah-tuh-**meñt**?
How long will it take to repair?	**Quanto tempo leva a arranjar?**
	kwuñtoo **teñ**poo **leh**-vuh arruñ**zhar**?
When will it be ready?	**Quando estará pronto?**
	kwuñdoo shtuh-**rah** pro**ñ**too?

Complaints

....

This is out of order	**Isto não funciona**
	eeshto nowñ foonss-**yo**nuh
The ... are out of order	**Os/As ... não funcionam**
	oosh/ush ... nowñ foonss-**yo**nowñ
light/heating	**a luz/o aquecimento**
	uh loosh/oo akuh-see**meñ**too
air conditioning	**o ar condicionado**
	oo ar koñdeess-yoo**nah**-doo
It's dirty	**Está sujo**
	shta **soo**zhoo
This isn't what I ordered	**Isto não é o que eu pedi**
	eeshtoo nowñ e oo kuh **ay**-oo puh-**dee**

82

To whom should I complain?	A quem me posso queixar?
	uh kayñ muh **poss**oo kay**shar**?
It's faulty	Tem um defeito
	tayñ ooñ duh-**fay**-too
I want a refund	Quero um reembolso
	kehroo ooñ ree-aym-**bol**soo
I want to return it	Quero devolver
	kehroo duh-vol**vehr**

Problems

· ·

Can you help me?	Pode-me ajudar?
	pod-muh azhoo**dar**?
I only speak a little Portuguese	Só falo um pouco de português
	so **fah**-loo ooñ **poh**koo duh poortoo-**gaysh**
Does anyone here speak English?	Há aqui alguém que fale inglês?
	a uh-**kee** al**gayñ** kuh **fah**-luh eeñ**glaysh**?
What's the matter?	Que se passa?
	kuh suh **pass**uh?
I would like to speak to whoever is in charge	Queria falar com o encarregado
	kree-uh fa**lar** koñ oo aynkuh-rray-**gah**-doo

> **Hotel desk** (p 48)

I'm lost	**Perdi-me**
	per**dee**-muh
How do I get to...?	**Como se vai a...?**
	koh-moo suh vy uh...?
I've missed...	**Perdi...**
	per**dee**...
my train	**o meu comboio**
	oo **may**oo koñ**boy**oo
my connection	**a minha ligação**
	uh **meen**-yuh leeguh-**sowñ**
I've missed my flight because there was a strike	**Perdi o meu voo porque havia uma greve**
	per**dee** oo **may**oo **voh**-oo **poor**kuh a**vee**-uh **oo**muh grev
The coach has left without me	**O autocarro partiu sem mim**
	oo owtoo-**karr**oo part**yoo** sayñ meeñ
Can you show me how this works?	**Pode-me mostrar como funciona isto?**
	pod-muh moosh**trar koh**-moo foonss-**yo**nuh **eesh**too?
I have lost my purse	**Perdi o meu porta-moedas**
	per**dee** oo **may**oo portuh-**mway**-dush
I need to get to...	**Preciso de ir a...**
	pre-**see**zoo deer uh...
Leave me alone!	**Deixe-me em paz!**
	day-shu-muh ayñ pash!
Go away!	**Vá-se embora!**
	vah-suh aym**boh**-ruh!

84

Emergencies

a polícia	uh poo**leess**-yuh	police
a ambulância uh uñboo**luñss**-yuh		ambulance
os bombeiros oos boñ**bay**-roosh		fire brigade
o banco do hospital oo **buñ**koo doo oshpee-**tahl**		casualty department

Help!	**Socorro!** soo**korr**oo!
Fire!	**Fogo!** **foh**-goo!
Can you help me?	**Pode-me ajudar?** **pod**-muh azhoo**dar**?
There's been an accident!	**Houve um acidente!** ohv ooñ asee**deñt**!
Someone is injured	**Há um ferido** a ooñ fe**ree**doo
Call...	**Chame...** sham...
the police	**a polícia** uh poo**leess**-yuh
an ambulance	**uma ambulância** **oo**muh amboo**luñss**-yuh

please	**por favor**
	poor fuh-**vor**
Where's the police station?	**Onde é a esquadra?**
	oñduh e uh **shkwah**-druh?
I want to report a theft	**Quero participar um roubo**
	kehroo purteesee**par** ooñ **roh**-boo
I've been attacked	**Fui agredido(a)**
	fwee agruh-**dee**-doo(uh)
Someone's stolen my...	**Roubaram-me...**
	roh-**bah**-rowñ-muh...
bag	**a mala**
	uh **mah**-luh
passport	**o passaporte**
	oo passuh-**port**
money	**o dinheiro**
	oo deen-**yay**-roo
My car's been broken into	**Assaltaram-me o carro**
	assal-**tah**-rowñ-muh oo **karr**oo
My car's been stolen	**Roubaram-me o carro**
	roh-**bah**-rowñ-muh oo **karr**oo
I've been raped	**Violaram-me**
	vyo**lah**-rowñ-muh
I am lost	**Perdi-me**
	per**dee**-muh
I want to speak to a policewoman	**Quero falar com uma mulher-polícia**
	kehroo fa**lar** koñ **oo**muh mool-**yehr** poo**leess**-yuh

I need to make an urgent telephone call	**Preciso de fazer uma chamada urgente** pre-**see**zoo duh fa**zehr oo**muh shuh-**mah**-duh oor**zheñt**
I need a report for my insurance	**Preciso de um relatório para o meu seguro** pre-**see**zoo dooñ rela**tor**yoo pro **may**oo se**goo**roo
I didn't know the speed limit	**Não sabia qual era o limite de velocidade** nowñ suh-**bee**-uh kwal **e**ruh oo lee**meet** duh vuh-loossee-**dahd**
How much is the fine?	**Quanto é a multa?** **kwuñ**too e uh **mool**tuh?
Where do I pay?	**Onde pago?** **oñ**duh **pah**-goo?
Do I have to pay straightaway?	**Tenho que pagar já?** **ten**-yoo kuh puh-**gar** zhah?

YOU MAY HEAR...

Posso ajudar? **poss**oo uzhoo**dar**?	Can I help you?
Passou a luz vermelha pa**ssoh** uh loosh ver**mel**-yuh	You went through a red light

Health

Pharmacy

a farmácia uh far**mass**-yuh	pharmacy
a farmácia de serviço uh far**mass**-yuh duh ser**vee**ssoo	duty chemist
a receita médica uh re**say**tuh **med**eekuh	prescription

Have you something for...?	**Tem alguma coisa para...?** tayñ al**goo**muh **koy**-zuh **pa**ruh...?
a headache	**a dor de cabeça** uh dor duh kuh-**beh**-suh
car sickness	**o enjoo** oo eñ**zhoh**-oo
diarrhoea	**a diarreia** uh dee-uh-**rray**uh
I have a rash	**Tenho uma irritação de pele** **ten**-yoo **oo**muh ee-rreetuh-**sowñ** duh pel

Is it safe for children?	**Pode-se dar às crianças?**
	pod-suh dar ash kree-**uñ**sush?
How much should I give?	**Quanto devo dar?**
	kwuñtoo **deh**-voo dar?

Três vezes por dia	Three times a day
antes/com/depois	before/with/after
das refeições	meals
traysh **veh**-zush poor **dee**-uh	
uñtsh/koñ/duh**poysh** dush	
ruh-fay-**soyñsh**	

Doctor

In Portuguese the possessive (my, his, her, etc) is generally not used with parts of the body, e.g.

| My head hurts | **Doi-me a cabeça** |
| My hands are dirty | **Tenho as mãos sujas** |

o hospital oo oshpee**tahl**	hospital
o banco (hospital)	casualty department
oo **buñ**koo oshpee**tahl**	
as horas de consulta	surgery hours
ush **o**rush duh koñ**sool**tuh	

Doctor

89

A **Não me sinto bem**
nowñ muh **seeñ**too bayñ
I don't feel well

B **Tem febre?**
tayñ **feb**ruh?
Do you have a temperature?

A **Não, mas doi-me aqui**
nowñ, mash **doy**-muh uh-**kee**
No, but I have a pain here

I need a doctor	**Preciso de um médico**
	pre-**see**zoo dooñ **med**eekoo
My son (daughter) is ill	**O meu filho(a) está doente**
	oo **may**oo **feel**-yoo(yuh) shta doo-**eñt**
(s)he has a temperature	**ele(a) tem febre**
	ayl(uh) tayñ **feb**ruh
I'm diabetic	**Sou diabético(a)**
	soh dee-uh-**bet**eekoo(uh)
I'm pregnant	**Estou grávida**
	shtoh **grah**-veeduh
I'm allergic to penicillin	**Sou alérgico(a) a penicilina**
	soh a**lehr**-zheekoo(uh) uh punee-see**lee**nuh
I'm on the pill	**Tomo a pílula**
	tomoo uh **peel**oo-luh
My blood group is...	**O meu grupo sanguíneo é...**
	oo **may**oo **groo**poo suñ**geen**-yoo e...

Health

90

Will he/she have to go to hospital?	**Tem que ir para o hospital?** tayñ kuh eer pro oshpee-**tahl**?
Will I have to pay?	**Tenho que pagar?** **ten**-yoo kuh puh-**gar**?
How much will it be?	**Quanto será?** **kwuñ**too suh-**rah**?
I need a receipt for the insurance	**Preciso de um recibo para o seguro** pre-**see**zoo dooñ ruh-**see**boo pro se**goo**roo

Tem que entrar no hospital tayñ kuh ayn**trar** noo oshpee-**tahl**	You will have to be admitted to hospital
Não é grave nowñ e grahv	It's not serious

Dentist

o chumbo	oo **shoom**boo	filling
a coroa	uh koo-**roh**-uh	crown
a dentadura postiça uh deñtuh-**doo**ruh poosh-**tee**suh		dentures

> **Emergencies** (p 85)

Dentist

I need a dentist	**Preciso de um dentista**
	pre-**see**zoo dooñ deñ**teesh**tuh
I have toothache	**Tenho uma dor de dentes**
	ten-yoo **oo**muh dor duh **deñtsh**
Can you do a temporary filling?	**Pode pôr um chumbo provisório?**
	pod por ooñ **shoom**boo provee-**zor**yoo?
It hurts (me)	**Doi-me doy**-muh
Can you give me something for the pain?	**Pode-me dar alguma coisa para a dor?**
	pod-muh dar al**goo**muh **koy**-zuh pra dor?
I think I have an abscess	**Creio que tenho um abcesso**
	krayoo kuh **ten**-yoo ooñ ab-**sess**oo
How much is it?	**Quanto custa?**
	kwuñtoo **koosh**tuh? .
I need a receipt for my insurance	**Preciso de um recibo para o seguro**
	pre-**see**zoo dooñ ruh-**see**boo pro se**goo**roo

YOU MAY HEAR...

É preciso arrancar e pre-**see**zoo arruñ**kar**	It has to come out
Vou-lhe dar uma injecção **vol**-yuh dar **oo**muh eeñzhe**sowñ**	I'm going to give you an injection

Health

Different types of travellers

Disabled travellers

What facilities do you have for disabled people?	Que instalaçãos tem para deficientes?
	kuh eeñshtaluh-**sownsh** tayñ **pa**ruh duh-feess-**yeñtsh**?
Are there any toilets for the disabled?	Há casas de banho especiais para deficientes?
	a **kah**-zush duh **bun**-yoo shpuh-ssee-**ysh pa**ruh duh-feess-**yeñtsh**?
Do you have any bedrooms on the ground floor?	Tem alguns quartos no rés-do-chão?
	tayñ al**goonsh kwar**toosh noo resh-doo-**showñ**?
Is there a lift?	Há elevador?
	a eeluh-vuh-**dor**?
Where is the lift?	Onde é o elevador?
	oñduh e oo eeluh-vuh-**dor**?
How many stairs are there?	Quantas escadas há?
	kwuñtush shkah-dush a?

Do you have wheelchairs?	**Tem cadeiras de rodas?** tayñ kuh-**day**-rush duh **rod**ush?
Can I visit ... with a wheelchair?	**Posso visitar ... com cadeira de rodas?** **poss**oo veezee**tar** ... koñ kuh-**day**-ruh duh **rod**ush?
Is there a reduction for disabled people?	**Há desconto para deficientes?** a dush**koñ**too **pa**ruh? duh-feess-**yeñtsh**
Is there somewhere I can sit down?	**Há algum sítio para me sentar?** a al**gooñ seet**yoo **pa**ruh muh señ**tar**?

With kids

- -

A child's ticket	**Um bilhete para criança** ooñ beel-**yet pa**ruh kree-**uñ**suh
He/She is ... years old	**Ele/Ela tem ... anos** ayl/**ay**luh tayñ ... **ah**-noosh
Is there a reduction for children?	**Há desconto para crianças?** a dush**koñ**too **pa**ruh kree-**uñ**sush?

94

Do you have a children's menu?	**Tem uma ementa para crianças?**
	tayñ **oo**muh ee**meñ**tuh pa**ruh** kree-**uñ**sush?
Is it OK to take children?	**É permitido levar crianças?**
	e permee**tee**-doo luh-**var** kree-**uñ**sush?
Do you have...?	**Tem...?**
	tayñ...?
a high chair	**uma cadeira alta**
	oomuh kuh-**day**-ruh **ahl**tuh
a cot	**um berço**
	oon **behr**-soo
I have two children	**Tenho dois filhos**
	ten-yoo doysh **feel**-yoosh
He/She is 10 years old	**Ele/Ela tem 10 anos**
	ayl/**ay**luh tayñ desh **ah**-noosh
Do you have any children?	**Tem filhos?**
	tayñ **feel**-yoosh?

With kids

> **Hotel** (p 46)

Reference

Alphabet

• •

The Portuguese alphabet is the same as the English, with the exception of three letters: K, W and Y. These letters are only used in foreign words that have come into use in Portuguese.

Como se escreve? **koh**-moo suh shkrev?	How do you spell it?
C de Carlos, L de Lisboa say duh **kar**loosh el duh leezh**boh**-uh	C for Carlos, L for Lisboa

A	ah	Alexandre	aluh-**shuñ**druh
B	bay	Bastos	**bash**-toosh
C	say	Carlos	**kar**loosh
D	day	Daniel	dan-**yel**
E	ay	Eduardo	eed**war**doo
F	ef	França	**fruñ**suh
G	zhay	Gabriel	gabree-**el**
H	a**gah**	Holanda	oh-**luñ**duh
I	ee	Itália	eetahl-yuh

J	**zhot**uh	José	zhoo**ze**
L	el	Lisboa	leezh**boh**-uh
M	em	Maria	ma**ree**-uh
N	en	Nicolau	neekoo-**lah**-oo
O	oh	Oscar	**osh**kar
P	pay	Paris	pa**reesh**
Q	kay	Quarto	**kwar**too
R	err	Ricardo	ree**kar**doo
S	ess	Susana	soo**zan**uh
T	tay	Teresa	tuh-**ray**-zuh
U	oo	Ulisses	oo**lee**sush
V	vay	Venezuela	vuh-nuh-**zway**-luh
X	sheesh	Xangai	shuñg-**gy**
Z	zay	Zebra	**zeb**ruh

Measurements and quantities

· ·

1 lb = approx. 0.5 kilo – 1 pint = approx. 0.5 litre

Liquids

1/2 litre...	**meio litro de...**
	mayoo **lee**troo duh...
a litre of...	**um litro de...**
	ooñ **lee**troo duh...
1/2 bottle of...	**meia garrafa de...**
	mayuh ga**rrah**-fuh duh ...

a bottle of...	**uma garrafa de...**
	oomuh ga**rrah**-fuh duh...
a glass of...	**um copo de...**
	ooñ **kop**oo duh...

Weights

100 grams of...	**cem gramas de...**
	sayñ **grah**-mush duh...
1/2 kilo of...	**meio quilo de...**
	mayoo **kee**loo duh...
1 kilo of...	**um quilo de...**
	ooñ **kee**loo duh...

Food

a slice of...	**uma fatia de...**
	oomuh fa**tee**-uh duh...
a portion of...	**uma porção de...**
	oomuh poor**sowñ** duh...
a dozen...	**uma dúzia de...**
	oomuh **doo**zee-uh duh...
a box of...	**uma caixa de...**
	oomuh **ky**-shuh duh...
a packet of...	**um pacote de...**
	ooñ pa**kot** duh...
a tin of...	**uma lata de...**
	oomuh **lah**-tuh duh...
a jar of...	**um boião de...**
	ooñ boy-**owñ** duh...

Miscellaneous

10 euros of...	**dez euros de...**	desh **eur**oosh duh...
a half	**metade**	muh-**tahd**
a quarter	**um quarto**	ooñ **kwar**too
ten per cent	**dez por cento**	desh poor **señ**too
more...	**mais...**	mysh...
less...	**menos...**	**meh**-noosh...
enough	**chega**	**sheh**-guh
double	**o dobro**	oo **doh**-broo
twice	**duas vezes**	**doo**-ush **veh**-zush
three times	**três vezes**	traysh **veh**-zush

Numbers

0	**zero**	**zehr**-oo
1	**um (uma)**	ooñ (**oo**muh)

2	**dois (duas)** doysh (**doo**-uz)
3	**três** traysh
4	**quatro kwat**roo
5	**cinco seeñ**koo
6	**seis** saysh
7	**sete** set
8	**oito oy**too
9	**nove** nov
10	**dez** desh
11	**onze** oñz
12	**doze** dohz
13	**treze** trezh
14	**catorze** ka**torz**
15	**quinze** keeñz
16	**dezasseis** dezuh-**saysh**
17	**dezassete** dezuh-**set**
18	**dezoito** de**zoy**too
19	**dezanove** dezuh-**nov**
20	**vinte** veeñt
21	**vinte e um** veeñtee-**ooñ**
22	**vinte e dois** veeñtee-**doysh**
23	**vinte e três** veeñtee-**traysh**
24	**vinte e quatro** veeñtee-**kwat**roo
25	**vinte e cinco** veeñtee-**seeñ**koo
26	**vinte e seis** veeñtee-**saysh**
27	**vinte e sete** veeñtee-**set**
28	**vinte e oito** veeñtee-**oy**too
29	**vinte e nove** veeñtee-**nov**
30	**trinta treeñ**tuh

40	**quarenta**	kwa**reñ**tuh
50	**cinquenta**	seeñ**kweñ**tuh
60	**sessenta**	se**señ**tuh
70	**setenta**	se**teñ**tuh
80	**oitenta**	oy**teñ**tuh
90	**noventa**	noo**veñ**tuh
100	**cem/cento**	sayñ/**señ**too
110	**cento e dez**	**señ**too ee desh
500	**quinhentos**	keen-**yeñ**toosh
1,000	**mil**	meel
2,000	**dois mil**	doysh meel
1 million	**um milhão**	ooñ meel-**yowñ**

1st	**primeiro** pree**may**roo		6th	**sexto** **sesh**-too	
2nd	**segundo** se**goon**doo		7th	**sétimo** **set**eemoo	
3rd	**terceiro** ter**say**roo		8th	**oitavo** oy**tah**-voo	
4th	**quarto** **kwar**too		9th	**nono** **noh**-noo	
5th	**quinto** **keeñ**too		10th	**décimo** **dess**eemoo	

Days and months

Days

Monday	**segunda-feira**	se**goon**duh **fay**ruh
Tuesday	**terça-feira**	**ter**suh-**fay**ruh
Wednesday	**quarta-feira**	**kwar**tuh-**fay**ruh
Thursday	**quinta-feira**	**keeñ**tuh-**fay**ruh
Friday	**sexta-feira**	**sesh**tuh-**fay**ruh
Saturday	**sábado**	**sah**-buh-doo
Sunday	**domingo**	do**meeñ**goo

Months

January	**janeiro**	zhuh**nay**roo
February	**fevereiro**	fuh-**vray**roo
March	**março**	**mar**soo
April	**abril**	a**breel**
May	**maio**	**my**-oo
June	**junho**	**zhoon**-yoo
July	**julho**	**zhool**-yoo
August	**agosto**	a**gosh**too
September	**setembro**	suh**teñ**broo
October	**outubro**	oh**too**broo
November	**novembro**	no**vayñ**-broo
December	**dezembro**	duh**zayñ**-broo

Seasons

spring	**a primavera**	uh preemuh-**vehr**uh
summer	**o verão**	oo vuh-**rowñ**
autumn	**o outono**	oo oh**toh**noo
winter	**o inverno**	oo eeñ**vehr**noo

What is today's date?	**Qual é a data hoje?**	kwal e uh **dah**-tuh ohzh?
It's the 5th of May 2008	**É cinco de maio de dois mil e oito**	e **seeñ**koo duh **my**-oo duh doysh meel ee **oy**too
on Saturday	**no sábado**	noo **sah**-buh-doo
on Saturdays	**aos sábados**	awsh **sah**-buh-doosh
every Saturday	**todos os sábados**	**toh**-doosh oosh **sah**-buh-doosh
this Saturday	**este sábado**	esht **sah**-buh-doo
next Saturday	**o próximo sábado**	oo **pross**eemoo **sah**-buh-doo
last Saturday	**o sábado passado**	oo **sah**-buh-doo puh-**sah**-doo
in June	**em Junho**	ayñ **zhoon**-yoo
at the beginning of...	**no princípio de...**	noo preeñ-**seep**-yoo duh...

at the end of...	**no fim de...**
	noo feeñ duh...
before the summer	**antes do verão**
	uñtsh doo vuh-**rowñ**
during the summer	**durante o verão**
	doo**ruñt** oo vuh-**rowñ**
after the summer	**depois do verão**
	duh-**poysh** doo vuh-**rowñ**

Time

● ●

The 24-hour clock is used a lot more than in Britain.
After 1200 midday, it continues: **1300 – treze
horas**, **1400 – catorze horas**, **1500 – quinze
horas**, etc, until **2400 – vinte e quatro horas
(meia-noite)**. With the 24-hour clock, the words
quarto (quarter) and **meia** (half) aren't used:

1315 (1.15 pm)	**treze e quinze**
1930 (7.30 pm)	**dezanove e trinta**
2245 (10.45 pm)	**vinte e duas e quarenta e cinco**

What time is it?	**Que horas são?**
	kee **or**ush sowñ?
am/pm	**da manhã/da tarde**
	duh mun-**yañ**/duh tard
It's ...	**São...**
	sowñ...

2 o'clock	**duas horas**
	doo-uz **or**ush
3 o'clock (etc.)	**três horas**
	trayz **or**ush
It's 1 o'clock	**É uma hora**
	e **oo**muh **or**uh
It's 1200 midday	**É meio-dia**
	e **may**oo **dee**-uh
At midnight	**À meia-noite**
	a **may**uh noyt
9	**nove horas**
	no**vee or**ush
9.10	**nove e dez**
	no**vee** desh
9.15	**nove e um quarto**
	no**vee** ooñ **kwar**too
9.20	**nove e vinte**
	no**vee** veeñt
9.30	**nove e trinta/nove e meia**
	no**vee treeñ**tuh/no**vee may**uh
9.35	**nove e trinta e cinco/**
	vinte e cinco para as dez
	no**vee treeñ**tuh ee **seeñ**koo/
	veeñ**tee seeñ**koo **pa**ruh ush desh
9.45	**dez menos um quarto/**
	nove e quarenta e cinco
	desh **meh**-nooz ooñ **kwar**too/
	no**vee** kwa**reñ**tuh ee **seeñ**koo

9.50	**dez para as dez/**
	nove e cinquenta
	desh **pa**ruh ush desh/
	no**vee** seeñk**weñ**tuh

Time phrases

....

When does it open/close?	**Quando abre/fecha?**
	kwuñdoo **ah**-bruh/**fay**shuh?
When does it begin/finish?	**Quando começa/acaba?**
	kwuñdoo koo**mess**uh/ a**kah**-buh?
at 3 o'clock	**às três horas**
	ash trayz **or**ush
before 3 o'clock	**antes das três**
	uñtsh dush tresh
after 3 o'clock	**depois das três**
	duh-**poysh** dush tresh
today	**hoje**
	ohzh
tonight	**esta noite**
	eshtuh noyt
tomorrow	**amanhã**
	amun-**yuñ**
yesterday	**ontem**
	oñtayñ

Eating out

Eating places

Tapas A popular and inexpensive venue is the Tapas bar – you'll find these wherever you go. It is a good way of trying out different foods.

Bar Serves drinks, coffee and snacks. Generally open all day. Look out for **pastéis de bacalhau** (cod cakes), **rissóis de camarão** (prawn rissoles) and **um prego** (a steak roll).

Cafetaria A cross between a bar and cake shop. It serves hot or cold drinks, cakes and light meals.

Casa de chá Literally a tea house, an elegant pâtisserie which serves a variety of drinks. Look out for **bolos**, mouth-watering Portuguese cakes, **torradas** (toast) and **sandes** (sandwiches made with white bread and often **queijo** (cheese), **fiambre** (ham) or **presunto** (cured ham)).

Pastelaria Pâtisserie or cake shop. Popular for snacks, soups and light meals. Lovely cakes.

Restaurante At restaurants, lunch is usually between 12.30 and 2.30 pm. Dinner starts at 7 or 7.30 pm and goes on until 9.30 or 10 pm.

Marisqueria Serves seafood as well as drinks.

Churrascaria Restaurant serving barbecued food, mainly chicken. Most are take-away places.

Cervejaria Beer house serving good lager and savouries. It generally offers a good menu, often specialising in seafood.

Tasca A small local tavern. Once cheap eating places, they are becoming gentrified.

Casa de pasto Simple, old-fashioned, restaurant usually offering good value meals at lunchtime.

In a bar/café

. . . .

If you want a small, strong black coffee ask for **um café** (also known as **uma bica**). A small, white coffee is **um garoto**. An ordinary white coffee is

um café com leite. A large (mug-sized) coffee is
um galão served in a tall glass. Tea is normally
served in a teapot, weak and without any milk.

a coffee	**um café**
	ooñ kuh-**fe**
a milky coffee	**um galão**
	ooñ ga**lowñ**
a lager	**uma cerveja**
	oomuh ser**vay**-zhuh
a (strong) tea...	**um chá (forte)...**
	ooñ shah (fort)...
with milk/lemon	**com leite/limão**
	koñ layt/lee**mowñ**
with toast	**com torradas**
	koñ too**rrah**-dush
for two	**para dois**
	paruh doysh
for me	**para mim**
	paruh meeñ
for him/her	**para ele/ela**
	paruh ayl/**ay**luh
for us	**para nós**
	paruh nosh
with ice, please	**com gelo, por favor**
	koñ **zhay**-loo, poor fuh-**vor**
very hot, please	**muito quente, por favor**
	mweeñtoo keñt, poor fuh-**vor**

a bottle of mineral water	**uma garrafa de água mineral**
	oomuh ga**rrah**-fuh **dahg**-wuh meenuh-**rahl**
sparkling/still	**com gás/sem gás**
	koñ gahs/sayñ gahs

Other drinks to try

um chocolate a chocolate, served hot **quente** or cold **frio**

um chá de limão boiling water poured over fresh lemon peel. A refreshing drink after a meal or at any time.

um batido de fruta fruit milkshake: try strawberry – **morango**

Reading the menu

Restaurants will have the menu displayed next to the entrance. If you don't want a full meal, it is better to go to a snack bar, **Pastelaria** (cake shop), **Cafetaria**, **Casa de chá** (tea house) or **Cervejaria** (beer house).

Pratos Combinados These are likely to consist of ham, egg, chips, fresh salad, perhaps, sausage and/or cheese and bread.

Pratos do Dia Literally, dishes of the day, these are generally more economical and readily served than the à la carte menu.

Ementa do Dia Set-price menu, with 3 courses (starter, meat or fish and dessert). May include wine.

Ementa Turística Set-price menu, as above, offering traditional dishes. The set-price menus may only be available for lunch.

Ementa	Menu (à la carte)
Entradas	Starters
Acepipes	Appetisers
Sopas	Soups
Peixe e Marisco	Fish and Shellfish
Pratos de Carne	Meat dishes
Ovos	Eggs
Acompanhamentos	Side dishes
Legumes	Vegetables
Saladas	Salads
Sobremesa	Desserts
Queijos	Cheeses

In a restaurant

In Portugal lunch at restaurants is usually between 12.30 and 2 pm. Dinner starts at 7 or 7.30 pm and goes on until 9.30 or 10 pm.

I'd like to book a table for ... people	**Queria reservar uma mesa para ... pessoas** **kree**-uh ruh-zer**var oo**muh **may**-zuh **pa**ruh ... puh-**so**-ush
for tonight...	**para esta noite...** **pa**ruh **esh**tuh noyt...
for tomorrow night...	**para amanhã à noite...** **pa**ruh amun-**yañ** a noyt...
at 8 pm	**às 8 horas** ash **oy**too **or**ush
The menu, please	**A ementa, por favor** uh ee**meñ**tuh, poor fuh-**vor**
What is the dish of the day?	**Qual é o prato do dia?** kwal e oo **prah**-too doo **dee**-uh?
Do you have a set-price menu?	**Tem a ementa do dia?** tayñ a ee**meñ**tuh doo **dee**-uh?
I'll have this	**Quero isto** **keh**roo **eesh**too
Can you recommend a local dish?	**Pode recomendar uma especialidade local?** pod ruh-koomeñ**dar oo**muh shpuh-syalee-**dahd** loo**kahl**?

112

Excuse me!	**Faz favor!**
	fash fuh-**vor**!
Please bring...	**Traga...**
	trah-guh...
more bread/ butter	**mais pão/manteiga**
	mysh powñ/muñ**tay**-guh
more water	**mais água**
	mysh **ahg**-wuh
a half portion	**meia dose**
	mayuh **doh**-zuh
another bottle	**outra garrafa**
	oh-truh ga**rrah**-fuh
the bill	**a conta**
	a **koñ**tuh
Is service included?	**O serviço está incluído?**
	oo ser**vee**soo shta eeñ-**klwee**doo?

Vegetarian

• •

There are very few vegetarian restaurants in Portugal, and those that do exist are located in the capital, in Porto and in some towns in the Algarve.

Are there any vegetarian restaurants here?	**Há algum restaurante vegetariano aqui?**
	a al**gooñ** rushtoh-**ruñt** veh-zhuh-tuh-**ryah**-noo uh-**kee**?

113

Do you have any vegetarian dishes?	**Tem algum prato vegetariano?**
	tayñ al**gooñ prah**-too veh-zhuh-tuh-**ryah**-noo?
Do you have any dishes without meat/fish?	**Tem pratos sem carne/peixe?**
	tayñ **prah**-toosh sayñ karn/paysh?
What fish dishes do you have?	**Que pratos de peixe tem?**
	kuh **prah**-toosh duh paysh tayñ?
I'd like pasta/rice...	**Queria massa/arroz...**
	kree-uh **mass**uh/a**rrosh**...
I don't like meat/fish	**Não gosto de carne/peixe**
	nowñ **gosh**too duh karn/paysh
What do you recommend?	**Que recomenda?**
	kuh ruh-koo**meñ**duh?
Is it made with vegetable stock?	**É feito com caldo vegetal?**
	e **fay**-too koñ **kahl**doo veh-zhuh-**tahl**?

Wines and spirits

● ●

A reasonably-priced wine is the **vinho de casa** (house wine), normally quite good and inexpensive.

The wine list, please	**A lista de vinhos, por favor**
	uh **leesh**tuh duh **veen**-yoosh, poor fuh-**vor**

Can you recommend a good wine?	**Pode recomendar um bom vinho?**
	pod ruh-koomeñ**dar** ooñ boñ **veen**-yoo?
A bottle.../ A carafe...	**Uma garrafa.../Um jarro...**
	oomuh ga**rrah**-fuh.../ ooñ **zharr**oo...
of the house wine	**de vinho da casa**
	duh **veen**-yoo duh **kah**-zuh
of red wine	**de vinho tinto**
	duh **veen**-yoo **teeñ**too
of white wine	**de vinho branco**
	duh **veen**-yoo **bruñ**koo
of rosé wine	**de vinho rosé**
	duh **veen**-yoo roh-**ze**
of 'green' wine	**de vinho verde**
	duh **veen**-yoo vehrd
of dry wine	**de vinho seco**
	duh **veen**-yoo **seh**-koo
of sweet wine	**de vinho doce**
	duh **veen**-yoo dohss
of a local wine	**de vinho da região**
	duh **veen**-yoo duh ruzh-**yowñ**
What liqueurs do you have?	**Que licores tem?**
	kuh lee-**korsh** tayñ?
A glass of port	**Um cálice de Porto**
	ooñ **kah**-leesuh duh **por**too
A glass of Boal (madeira)	**Um cálice de Boal**
	ooñ **kah**-leesuh duh boo-**ahl**

Port wines offer a wide variety of styles, making them suitable for all occasions and also for serving with food. The main types are:

White (which can be sweet or dry, so check the label). Good on its own or as an aperitif. It should be chilled and can be made into a long drink with a little ice and a twist of lemon.

Ruby is a blend of young ports, ready to drink, spicy and fruity. Sweet and ruby in colour. No need to decant.

Tawny is a blend from various harvests. It has a rich amber colour, a long finish and complex aroma. Look for labels indicating its age (10, 20, 30 years old). It is ready to drink and does not need decanting. This is the most popular style.

Vintage Port is a wine from an exceptional declared harvest. Matured in wood for two or three years, it is bottled and continues to mature, for at least 10 years, or much longer. It must be decanted. It is dark and rich, becoming softer and more complex as it ages. There are intermediate styles (LBV, for example). The label should help.

Madeira wines, like ports, can be served as an aperitif, for dessert or on any other occasion. The four categories are:

Sercial quite dry and pale
Verdelho less dry and slightly darker than **Sercial**
Boal richer-coloured and sweeter
Malvasia dark, very perfumed, full-bodied and
  very sweet

Whatever their category, these wines are always very aromatic and complex. The drier styles should be served chilled.

Wines and spirits

Menu reader

...**à caçadora** hunter-style (poultry or game marinated in wine and garlic)
...**à jardineira** garden-style with vegetables such as green beans and carrots
...**à lagareiro** baked dish made with lots of olive oil
...**à marinheira** with white wine, onions and parsley
...**à portuguesa** Portuguese fashion, i.e. with tomato sauce

abacate avocado
abacaxi pineapple
abóbora pumpkin
açafrão saffron
acelga swiss chard
acepipes appetisers
acompanhamentos side dishes
açorda typical Portuguese dish with bread
  açorda com peixe frito thick bread soup accompanying fried fish
  açorda de alho bread soup with garlic and beaten egg (generally served with fried fish)
  açorda de marisco thick bread soup with shellfish and a beaten egg, typical of the Lisbon area

açúcar sugar
adocicado slightly sweet
agrião watercress
água water
  água mineral com gás sparkling mineral water
  água mineral sem gás still mineral water
aguardente brandy
aipo celery
albardado in batter
alcachofra artichoke
alface lettuce
alho garlic
alho francês leek
almoço lunch
almôndegas meatballs
alperces apricots
amargo bitter
amarguinha bitter-almond liqueur
amêijoas clams
  amêijoas à Bulhão Pato clams with garlic and
  coriander
  amêijoas ao natural natural steamed clams with
  herbs and lemon butter
ameixa plum
  ameixa seca prune
amêndoas almonds
amendoim peanut
amora blackberry
ananás pineapple

aniz aniseed liqueur
arenque herring
arjamolho kind of gazpacho soup
arroz branco plain rice
  arroz de Cabidela chicken or rabbit highly seasoned risotto
  arroz de ervilhas pea rice
  arroz de frango chicken with rice
  arroz de lampreia lamprey with rice
  arroz de manteiga rice with butter
  arroz doce rice pudding
assado roasted, baked
  assado no forno oven-roasted
  assado no espeto spit roasted
atum tuna fish
  atum assado braised tuna with onions and tomatoes
  atum de cebolada tuna steak with onions and tomato sauce
  atum salpresado salted tuna dish
aveia oats
avelã hazelnut
aves fowl
azeda sorrel
azedo sour
azeite olive oil
azeitonas olives

bacalhau salt cod

  bacalhau à Brás traditional dish with salt cod, onion and potatoes all bound with scrambled eggs

  bacalhau à Gomes de Sá good salt cod dish with layers of potatoes, onions and boiled eggs, laced with olive oil and baked

  bacalhau com natas salt cod in cream sauce au gratin

  bacalhau com todos salt cod poached with potatoes and vegetables

  bacalhau na brasa salt cod grilled on charcoal, served with olive oil

barriga de freira a sweet made with yolks and sugar, slightly caramelised

batata potato

  batata doce sweet potato

  batatas a murro potatoes baked in their own skins then soaked in olive oil

  batatas fritas chips

  batatas cozidas boiled potatoes

batido de fruta fruit milkshake

baunilha vanilla

bebida drink

bem passado well done

berbigão cockle

beringela aubergine

besugo sea bream

beterraba beetroot

bica small strong black coffee

bifana hot meat, normally pork tenderloin in a roll

bife steak (and chips and perhaps fried egg)

  bife à café steak in cream sauce topped with a fried egg (with chips)

bifinhos de vitela veal fillet with Madeira sauce

biscoitos cookies

bitoque small steak with fried egg and chips

bola layered bread and cured meat pie

  bola de Berlim doughnut

bolachas biscuits

  bolachas de água e sal water biscuits (crackers)

boleimas cakes with a bread dough base

bolinhos de bacalhau cod croquettes

bolo caseiro homemade cake

bolo de chocolate chocolate cake

bolo de mel honey cake

bolo podre dark cake made with honey, olive oil and spices

borracho young pigeon

borrego lamb

branco white

broa a crusty rustic maize bread

brócolos broccoli

bucho pork haggis

cabrito kid

  cabrito assado roast kid with a spiced marinade

  cabrito montês roebuck

caça game

cacau cocoa

cachorro hotdog

cachucho small sea bream

café coffee

  bica small, strong black coffee (espresso)

  carioca small but slightly weaker black coffee

  com leite white coffee

  duplo large cup of black coffee

  frio iced coffee

  galão large white coffee served in a tall glass

  garoto small white coffee

caju cashew nut

caldeirada fish stew

  caldeirada à fragateira seafood stew, as prepared by fishermen

  caldeirada de enguias eel stew

caldo broth

  caldo verde green broth, made with shredded kale and potatoes with **chouriço** and olive oil

camarões shrimps

caneca medium-sized beer glass

canela cinnamon

canja chicken soup, thickened with rice or small pasta and chicken pieces

capilé drink with iced coffee, lemon rind and sugar

caracóis snails (small, cooked in a tasty broth)

caranguejo crab

carapau horse mackerel

caril curry

carioca small weak coffee
carioca de limão lemon infusion
carne meat
  carne assada roast meat
  carne de porco à alentejana highly seasoned
  pork dish with clams, typical of the Alentejo
carneiro mutton
carnes frias cold meats
carta dos vinhos wine list
casa de chá tea-house
casa de pasto restaurant serving cheap, homely
  meals
castanha chestnut
cataplana meat, fish or shellfish dish cooked with
  potatoes and a tomato sauce in a cataplana pot
cavala mackerel
cebola onion
cenoura carrot
cereja cherry
cerveja beer/lager
  cerveja à pressão draught beer
  cerveja em garrafa bottled beer
  cerveja preta dark ale
cervejaria beer house, serving food
chá tea
  chá com leite tea with milk
  chá com limão tea with lemon
  chá forte strong tea
  chá de ervas/tisana herb tea

chanfana rich lamb/kid stew
cherne species of grouper with dark skin
chicória endive
chila type of pumpkin made into jam
chispalhada pig's trotters stew
chispe com feijão trotters with beans, cured meats and vegetables
chocolate chocolate
chocos com tinta cuttlefish in its own ink
choquinhos squid
  choquinhos com tinta squid in its ink
chouriço spicy smoked sausage
chuchu marrow
churrasco barbecued/cooked on charcoal
churrasqueira restaurant specialising in **frango à piri-piri** (chicken with chilli)
coco coconut
codorniz quail
coelho rabbit
coentrada with fresh coriander
coentros fresh coriander
cogumelos mushrooms
colorau sweet paprika
cominho cumin seed
compota jam or compote
congro conger eel
conhaque cognac
conta bill
copo glass

coração heart
cordeiro lamb
costeletas de porco pork chops
couve cabbage
  couve-de-bruxelas brussels sprouts
  couve-flor cauliflower
  couve-lombarda savoy cabbage
  couve-roxa red cabbage
cozido boiled or poached
  cozido à Madeirense boiled Madeira-style pork
  and vegetables, with pumpkin and couscous
cravinhos cloves
creme custard
criação fowl
croissants com fiambre ham-filled croissants
croissants recheados filled croissants
croquetes de carne meat croquettes
cru raw
cuba livre rum and Coke

damasco apricot
digestivo digestive, e.g. brandy
dobrada tripe
doce sweet
  doces de amêndoa marzipan sweets
  doce de fruta jam
  doce de laranja marmalade
dourada sea bream

eirós large eel

ementa menu

empadão de batata shepherd's pie

empadas small chicken or veal pies

enguias fritas fried eels

ensopado fish or meat stew served on bread slices

ensopado de borrego rich lamb stew served on bread slices

entradas starters

entrecosto entrecôte steak

erva-doce aniseed

ervilhas peas

  ervilhas com paio e ovos peas with garlic sausage and poached eggs

escabeche a sauce containing vinegar, normally served with cold fried fish

escalfado poached

  ovo escalfado poached egg

espada the name given in Madeira to **peixe espada** (scabbard fish)

espadarte swordfish

esparguete spaghetti

espargos asparagus

esparregado spinach purée with garlic

especiarias spices

espetada kebab

esplanada open-air restaurant/café

espinafre spinach

estragão tarragon

estufado braised
  carne estufada braised meat
esturjão sturgeon
extra-seco extra-dry

farinha flour
farinheira sausage made with flour and pork fat
fartes de batata square cakes of sweet potato
  purée with spices and almonds
fataça grey mullet
fatias de Tomar sponge slices served in a light syrup
fatias douradas slices of bread dipped in egg, fried
  and covered with sugar and cinnamon
favada à portuguesa broad beans cooked with
  smoked meats, onions and coriander
favas broad beans
febras thin slices of roast pork
  febras de porco à alentejana pork fillet with
  onions, **chouriço** and bacon
feijão beans
  feijão encarnado red beans
  feijão frade black-eyed beans
  feijão guisado beans stewed with bacon in a
  tomato sauce
  feijão preto black beans
  feijão verde cozido boiled French beans
feijoada bean stew with pork meat and **chouriço**
fiambre ham
fígado liver

fígado de coentrada pork liver with coriander
fígado de galinha chicken liver
fígado de porco de cebolada pork liver with onions
figos figs
filetes de pescada hake fillet in batter
folhados de carne meat puff-pastries
frango young chicken
  frango à piri-piri barbecued tender chicken with chilli
  frango assado roast tender chicken
  fresco/a cold or fresh
  uma cerveja muito fresca a very cool beer
fressura de porco guisada pork offal casserole
fricassé meat or fish (generally chicken) served with an egg and lemon sauce
frio cold
fritada de peixe deep-fried mixed fish
frito fried
fruta fruit
fumado smoked
fundo de alcachofra artichoke heart

galinha chicken
galinhola woodcock
galão milky coffee served in a large glass
gambas large prawns
  gambas na chapa large prawns cooked on the hot plate
ganso goose

garoto small white coffee
garoupa grouper
gasosa soft drink with gas
gaspacho cold soup with finely cut vegetables
gelado ice-cream
geleia jelly
gelo ice
gengibre ginger
gim gin
ginjinha morello-cherry liqueur typical of Portugal
girafa beer glass (equivalent to a pint)
goiaba guava
granizado de café iced coffee
grão chickpeas
grelhado grilled
groselha (red)currant
guisado stewed

hortaliça generic name given to vegetables
  sopa de hortaliça vegetable soup
hortelã mint
  chá de hortelã mint tea
hortelã-pimenta peppermint

imperial small beer glass
incluído included
inhame yam
iscas traditional pork liver dish with wine and garlic

jardineira mixed vegetables
jarro carafe
javali wild boar
jeropiga fortified dessert wine

lagosta lobster
lagostim-do-rio freshwater crayfish
lagostins king prawns
lampreia lamprey (an eel-like fish)
lanche afternoon snack consisting of tea and cakes
  or buttered toast
lapas limpets, popular in Madeira and the Azores
  lapas Afonso limpets served with an onion sauce
laranja orange
  laranja descascada peeled orange, normally
  served with a sprinkle of sugar
laranjada fizzy orange
  laranjada engarrafada bottled orange juice
lavagante species of lobster
lebre hare
legumes vegetables
leite milk
  leite-creme crème brûlée
lentilha lentil
licor de leite milk liqueur
  licor de tangerina mandarin liqueur
lima lime
limão lemon
limonada lemonade

língua tongue
　língua estufada braised tongue
linguado sole
linguiça pork sausage with paprika
lista dos vinhos wine list
lombinho de porco pork loin
lombo de porco pork fillet
louro bay leaf
lulas squid
　lulas à Algarvia squid in garlic, Algarve style
　lulas guisadas stewed squid
　lulas recheadas squid stuffed with rice

maçã apple
　maçã assada large baked russet apple
maçapão marzipan
macarrão macaroni
macedónia de frutas mixed fruit salad
malagueta hot pepper
mal passado rare
manjar celeste sweet made with eggs,
　breadcrumbs, almonds and sugar
manjericão basil
manteiga butter
mãozinhas de vitela guisadas stewed calves'
　trotters
maracujá passion fruit
marinado/a marinated
marisco shellfish

marisqueira a restaurant or bar specialising in
  shellfish
marmelada quince jam – excellent with cheese
marmelo quince, a popular fruit, often baked
massa pasta
medalhão medallion
medronheira strawberry-tree fruit liqueur
meia-dose half-portion
meia garrafa half bottle
meio-doce medium-sweet
meio-seco medium-dry
mel honey
mel de cana molasses
melancia watermelon
melão melon
merenda afternoon snack
merendinha pastry filled with **chouriço** or
  presunto (ham)
mero red grouper fish
mexilhões mussels
migas bread cooked with well-seasoned
  ingredients to form a kind of omelette
  migas à alentejana thick bread soup with pork
  meat and garlic
  migas de pão de milho thick maize bread soup
  with olive oil and garlic
mil-folhas millefeuille (custard pastry)
milho corn (maize)
milho doce sweetcorn

miolos brains
misto mixed
molho sauce
  molho de caril curry sauce
  molho de escabeche a sauce containing vinegar,
  normally served with cold fried fish
morangos strawberries
morcela spicy black pudding
morgado de figo dried pressed figs with spices
moscatel de Setúbal medium-sweet muscat wine
mostarda mustard

nabiça turnip greens
nabo turnip
...na brasa char-grilled
...na cataplana stewed in cataplana vessel (typical
  double-wok pot used in the Alentejo and Algarve)
...na frigideira sautéed or fried
natas cream
  nata batida whipped cream
...no espeto kebab/on the spit
...no forno roasted or cooked in the oven
nozes walnuts

óleo vegetable oil
omeleta de cogumelos mushroom omelette
omeleta de fiambre ham omelette
omeleta simples plain omelette
ostras oysters

ouriço-do-mar sea-urchin
ovas fish roe
ovos eggs
  ovos cozidos boiled eggs
  ovos escalfados poached eggs
  ovos estrelados fried eggs
  ovos mexidos scrambled eggs

paio thick smoked sausage made with lean meat
palha de Abrantes sweet made with eggs
panados slices of meat coated in egg and
  breadcrumbs and fried
pão bread
  pão de centeio rye bread
  pão de forma sliced bread for toast
  pão-de-ló light sponge cake
  pão de milho maize bread
  pão de queijo Brazilian cheese and maize snack
  pão saloio country-style bread
pãozinho roll
papaia papaya
papas polenta soup
  papas de milho doces sweet polenta
papo seco bread roll
papos de anjo small egg cakes with syrup
pargo red bream
parrilhada grilled fish
passas de uva raisins
pastéis tarts, cakes, pasties

pastéis de bacalhau salt cod cakes
pastéis de carne meat pasties
pastéis de feijão tarts made with beans, eggs and almonds
pastel de massa tenra meat pasty
pataniscas (de bacalhau) salt cod fritters
paté de fígado liver pâté
pato duck
pé de porco com feijão pigs' trotters with beans
peito breast
peixe fish
  peixe assado/cozido/frito/grelhado baked/poached/fried/grilled fish
  peixe e marisco fish and shellfish
  peixe espada scabbard fish
peixe-galo John Dory
peixinhos da horta French beans fried in batter
pepino cucumber
pequeno almoço breakfast
pêra pear
percebes barnacles, highly prized shellfish
perdiz partridge
perna leg
pernil ham
peru turkey
pescada hake
  pescada com todos hake poached with potatoes and vegetables
pêssego peach

pêssego careca nectarine
petisco savoury or snack
pezinhos de porco de coentrada pork trotters
  with coriander and garlic
picante spicy
pimenta pepper (spice)
pimentos peppers
pinhão pine kernel
pinhoada pinenut brittle
pinhões peanuts
polvo octopus
pombo pigeon
porco pork
  porco à alentejana traditional dish with pork,
  clams and herbs
  porco assado roast pork
  porco preta black pork
posta à mirandesa spit-roasted veal, Miranda-style
pouco picante mild
prato dish
  prato do dia dish of the day
  prato principal main dish
  pratos de carne meat dishes
preço price
pregado turbot
prego steak in a roll
  prego com fiambre steak with sliced ham
  prego no pão steak roll
  prego no prato steak with fried egg and chips

presunto cured ham

preta dark

pudim Abade de Priscos rich egg pudding flavoured with port and lemon

pudim de bacalhau salt cod loaf served with tomato sauce

pudim de pão bread pudding

pudim de queijo cheese pudding

pudim de requeijão ricotta-type cheese pudding

pudim flan crème caramel

pudim Molotov egg-white pudding with egg sauce or caramel

queijadas de Évora cheese tarts made with cheese from ewes' milk

queijadas de requeijão ricotta-type cheese tarts

queijinhos de amêndoa little almond cheeses

queijinhos do céu egg yolk and sugar sweets

queijinhos frescos small fresh cheeses

queijinhos secos small dried cheeses

queijo cheese

  queijo cabreiro goats' cheese

  queijo cardiga cheese made from ewes' and goats' milk

  queijo de cabra goats' cheese

  queijo de ovelha small, dried ewes' milk cheeses

quente hot

quiabo okra

rabanada french toast
rabanete radish
raia skate
rancho a substantial soup
recheado com... stuffed/filled with...
recheio stuffing
repolho cabbage
requeijão fresh curd cheese resembling ricotta
rim (rins) kidney
rissóis de camarão/peixe shrimp or fish rissoles
robalo sea bass
rojões crisp pieces of marinated pork
romas pomegranate

sal salt
salada salad
  salada de feijão frade black-eyed bean salad,
  with boiled egg, olive oil and seasonings
  salada de polvo a starter with cold octopus,
  seasoned with olive oil, coriander, onion and vinegar
salgados savouries (snacks)
salmão salmon
  salmão fumado smoked salmon
salmonetes grelhados grilled red mullet in a
  butter and lemon sauce
saloio small cheese made from ewes' or goats'
  milk, often served as a pre-starter
salpicão slices of large **chouriço**
salsa parsley

139

salsichas sausages
salteado sautéed
salva sage
sandes sandwich
  sandes de lombo steak sandwich
  sandes mista ham and cheese sandwich
santola spider crab
sapateira crab (generally dressed)
sarda mackerel
sardinhas assadas char-grilled sardines
sardinhas na telha oven-baked sardines cooked
  on a roof tile with olive oil and seasoning
sável shad
seco dry
sericaia baked custard with cinnamon
serpa a type of ewes' milk cheese
serra a creamy cheese made from ewes' milk
serviço incluído service included
sidra cider
simples neat (as in 'neat whisky')
sobremesas desserts
solha plaice
sonho doughnut-type small fried cake, dipped in
  sugar and cinnamon
sopa soup
  sopa à alentejana soup Alentejo-style, made
  with chunks of bread, olive oil, fresh coriander and
  garlic, topped with poached egg

sopa de cabeça de peixe fish head soup with tomatoes, potatoes, stale bread and seasonings
sopa de camarão prawn soup
sopa de castanhas piladas hearty soup made with dried chestnuts, beans and rice
sopa de ervilhas pea soup
sopa de espinafres spinach soup
sopa de feijão bean soup with vegetables
sopa de grão chickpea soup
sopa de legumes vegetable soup
sopa de marisco shellfish soup
sopa de pedra a rich soup with lots of meat, beans and vegetables
sopa de rabo de boi oxtail soup
sopa do dia soup of the day
sopa dos campinos salt cod and tomato soup
sopa dourada dessert made with egg yolks
sopa seca thick bread soup with meat
sorvete sorbet
sumo de fruta fruit juice
suspiros meringues

tainha grey mullet
tâmara date
tamboril monkfish
tangerina mandarin
tarte de amêndoa almond tart
tarte de limão lemon tart
tarte de maçã apple tart

tasca/tasquinha small taverna serving cheap food and drink

tempero seasoning

tenro tender

tibornas slices of freshly baked bread sprinkled with coarse sea salt and olive oil

tigeladas de Abrantes individually baked custards

tinto red wine

tisana herbal tea

tisana de camomila camomile tea

tisana de Lúcia-Lima vervaine tea

tomate tomato

toranja grapefruit

tornedó prime cut of beef

torradas toast

torta swiss roll

torta de laranja orange sponge roll

torta de Viana sponge roll filled with egg custard

tosta toasted sandwich

tosta mista ham and cheese toasted sandwich

toucinho bacon

toucinho do céu egg and almond pudding

tremoços lupin seeds often eaten with beer

tripas à moda do Porto tripe stew with beans and various meats, Porto-style

trufa truffle

truta trout

trutas à moda do Minho trout cooked in wine and rich seasonings

truta de Barroso fried trout stuffed with ham
tutano marrow

uísque whisky
uvas grapes

vaca beef
vagens runner beans
variado assorted
vermute vermouth
vieira scallop
vinagre vinegar
vinha d'alhos marinated in wine and garlic
vinho abafado locally made fortified wine
vinho adamado sweet wine
vinho branco white wine
vinho branco seco dry white wine
vinho da casa house wine
vinho espumante sparkling wine
vinho tinto red wine
vinho verde dry, sparkling 'green' wine made with
  slightly unripe grapes from the Minho region
vinhos espumantes sparkling wines
vitela veal
  vitela no espeto veal cooked on the spit

xarope syrup
xerez sherry

Grammar

Nouns

• •

Portuguese nouns are masculine or feminine, and their gender is shown by the words for 'the' (**o/a**) and 'a' (**um/uma**) used before them (articles):

	masculine	feminine
singular	**o castelo** the castle **um castelo** a castle	**a mesa** the table **uma mesa** a table
plural	**os castelos** the castles **(uns) castelos** (some) castles	**as mesas** the tables **(umas) mesas** (some) tables

Nouns ending in -**o** or -**or** are usually masculine. Those ending in -**a**, -**agem**, -**dade** and -**tude** tend to be feminine. Nouns ending in a vowel form the plural by adding -**s**, while those ending in a consonant usually add -**es**. Words ending in -**m** change to -**ns**, and words ending in -**l**, change to -**is**.

Note: When used after the words **a** (to), **de** (of), **em** (in) and **por** (by), articles (and many other words) contract:

a + as = às ash		to the
de + um = dum dooñ		of a
em + uma = numa noo-muh		to a
por + os = pelos peh-loosh		by the

This, that, these, those...

These depend on the gender and number of the noun they represent:

este rapaz	**esta rapariga**
this boy	this girl
estes rapazes	**estas raparigas**
these boys	these girls
esse rapaz	**essa rapariga**
that boy	that girl
esses rapazes	**essas raparigas**
those boys	those girls
aquele rapaz	**aquela rapariga**
that boy (over there)	that girl (over there)
aqueles rapazes	**aquelas raparigas**
those boys (over there)	those girls (over there)

Adjectives

Portuguese adjectives normally follow the nouns they describe and reflect the gender in e.g. **a maçã verde** the green apple.

Some exceptions which go before the noun are:

muito much, many	**último** last
pouco little, not much	**bom** good
tanto so much, so many	**nenhum** no, not any
primeiro first	**grande** great, big

To make an adjective feminine, **-o** endings change to **-a**, and **-or** and **-ês** change to **-ora** and **-esa**. Otherwise they generally have the same form for both genders.

masculine	feminine
o livro vermelho the red book	**a saia vermelha** the red skirt
o homem falador the talkative man	**a mulher faladora** the talkative woman

To make adjectives plural, follow the rules given for nouns.

My, your, his, her...

These words depend on the gender and number of the noun and not the sex of the 'owner'.

	with masc./fem	with plural nouns
my	o meu/a minha	os meus/ as minhas
his/her/its/your	o seu/a sua	os seus/as suas
our	o nosso/a nossa	os nossos/ as nossas
your	o vosso/a vossa	os vossos/ as vossas
their/your	o seu/a sua	os seus/as suas

Note: Since **o seu**, **a sua**, etc can mean 'his', 'her', 'your', etc, the forms (**dele**, **dela**, **deles** and **delas**) are often used to avoid confusion:

os livros dela   her books
os livros deles   their books

Pronouns

subject		object	
I	eu **ay**-oo	me	me muh
you (informal)	tu too	you (informal)	te teh
you	você voh-**say**	you	o/a oo/uh
he	ele ayl	him	o oo
she	ela **ay**luh	her	a uh
it	ele/ela ayl/**ay**luh	it	o/a oo/uh
we	nós nosh	us	nos noosh
you	vós vosh	you	vos voosh
they (masc.)	eles **ay**lush	them (masc.)	os oosh
they (fem.)	elas **el**ush	them (fem.)	as ush
you (informal)	vocês voh-**saysh**	you (informal)	os/as oosh/ush

Notes

1. YOU The polite way of addressing someone would be with **o senhor** or **a senhora**, using the (s)he form of the verb and the object pronoun **o/a**. The semi-formal 'you' is **você** and the informal 'you' is **tu** (as in French).

2. Subject pronouns are normally not used except for emphasis or to avoid confusion:

148

eu vou para Lisboa e ele vai para Coimbra
I'm going to Lisbon and he's going to Coimbra

3. Object pronouns are usually placed after the verb and joined with a hyphen:

vejo-o	I see him

However, in sentences beginning with a 'question' or 'negative' word, the pronoun goes in front of the verb:

quando o viu?	when did you see him?
não o vi	I did not see him

In phrases beginning with 'that', 'who', etc (subordinate clauses), the pronoun also precedes the verb:

sei que o viu	I know that you saw him
o homem que o viu	the man who saw him

4. ME **also** = to me and **nos** = to us, but **lhe** = to him/to her/to it/to you (formal), **te** = to you (informal) and **lhes** = to them/to you.

Verbs

• •

Portuguese regular verbs follow one of three patterns of endings. Examples of the present and past tenses are given overleaf.

Present tense

Verbs ending in -**ar**

cant**ar**	**to sing**
canto	I sing
cantas	you sing
canta	(s)he/it sings/you sing
cantamos	we sing
cantais	you sing
cantam	they/you sing

Verbs ending in -**er**

com**er**	**to eat**
como	I eat
comes	you eat
come	(s)he/it eats/you eat
comemos	we eat
comeis	you eat
comem	they/you eat

Verbs ending in -**ir**

part**ir**	**to leave**
parto	I leave
partes	you leave
parte	(s)he/it leaves/you leave
partimos	we leave
partis	you leave
partem	they/you leave

Grammar

Past tense

Verbs ending in **-ar**

cantei	I sang
cantaste	you sang
cantou	(s)he/it/you sang
cantámos	we sang
cantastes	you sang
cantaram	they/you sang

Verbs ending in **-er**

comi	I ate
comeste	you ate
comeu	(s)he/it/you ate
comemos	we ate
comestes	you ate
comeram	they/you ate

Verbs ending in **-ir**

parti	I left
partiste	you left
partiu	(s)he/it/you left
partimos	we left
partistes	you left
partiram	they/you left

Irregular verbs don't follow a pattern, so you need to learn their endings. Four of the most common verbs are irregular:

ser	**to be**	estar	**to be**
sou	I am	estou	I am
és	you are	estás	you are
é	(s)he/it is/	está	(s)he/it is/
	you are		you are
somos	we are	estamos	we are
sois	you are	estais	you are
são	they/you are	estão	they/you are

ter	**to have**	ir	**to go**
tenho	I have	vou	I go
tens	you have	vais	you go
tem	(s)he/it has/	vai	(s)he/it goes/
	you have		you go
temos	we have	vamos	we go
tendes	you have	ides	you go
têm	they/you have	vão	they/you go

Note: **Ser** and **estar** both mean 'to be'.

Ser is used to describe a permanent place or state:

| **sou inglês** | I am English |
| **é uma praia** | it is a beach |

Estar is used to describe a temporary state or where something is located:

| **como está?** | how are you? |
| **onde está o livro?** | where is the book? |

Public holidays

January 1	**Ano Novo** New Year's Day
February/March*	**Carnaval** Mardi Gras, Shrove Tuesday
March/April*	**Sexta-Feira Santa** Good Friday
March/April*	**Páscoa** Easter Sunday
April 25	**Dia da Liberdade** 'Freedom Day'
May 1	**Dia do Trabalhador** Labour Day
May/June*	**Corpo de Deus** Corpus Christi
June 10	**Dia de Portugal** Portugal Day
August 15	**Assunção** Assumption of Mary
October 5	**Implantação da República** Republic Day
November 1	**Todos os Santos** All Saints' Day
December 1	**Restauração da Independência** Restoration of Independence (1640)
December 8	**Imaculada Conceição de Maria** Immaculate Conception of Mary
December 25	**Natal** Christmas Day

* date varies

English – Portuguese

A

a	um (uma)	ooñ (oomuh)
able: to be able (to)	poder	poodehr
about (roughly)	mais ou menos	mysh oh meh-noosh
about ten o'clock	por volta das dez	poor voltuh dush desh
above	acima de	uh-see-muh duh
to accept	aceitar	uh-say-tar
access (approve of)	aprovar	uh-proovar
	o acesso	uh-sessoo
accident	o acidente	aseedeñt
accommodation	o alojamento	alozhuh-meñto
account (bill)	a conta	koñtuh
(in bank)	a conta bancária	koñtuh buñkar-yuh
to ache	doer	doo-ehr
my head aches	dói-me a cabeça	doy-muh uh kuh-beh-suh
address	a morada	moo-rah-duh
admission charge/fee	o preço de entrada	pray-soo duh eñ-trah-duh
adult	o/a adulto(a)	uhdooltoo(uh)
advance: in advance	antecipadamente	uñtessee-pah-duh-meñt
afraid: to be afraid of	ter medo de	tehr meh-doo duh
after	depois	duh-poysh
afternoon	a tarde	tard
again	outra vez	oh-truh vesh
age	a idade	eedahd
agency	a agência	uh-zhañ-syuh
ago: 2 days ago	há 2 dias	a doysh dee-ush
to agree	concordar	koñkordar
AIDS	a SIDA	seeduh
air conditioning	o ar condicionado	o ar koñdeess-yoonah-doo
airline	a linha aérea	leen-yuh
airplane	o avião	av-ehreh-uh
airport	o aeroporto	ayroo-portoo

English	Portuguese	pronunciation	English	Portuguese	pronunciation
air ticket	o bilhete de avião	beel-**yet** duh av-**yowñ**	alone	sozinho(a)	soh-**zeen**-yoo(uh)
alarm	o alarme	alarmuh	already	já	zhah
alarm clock	o despertador	deesh-pehrtuh-**dor**	also	também	tuñ**bayñ**
			always	sempre	**sayñ**pruh
alcohol	o álcool	**ahl**kol	a.m.	da manhã	duh mun-**yañ**
alcohol-free	sem álcool	sayñ **ahl**kol	ambulance	a ambulância	amboo**luñss**-yuh
alcoholic adj	alcoólico(a)	al-**koleekoo**(uh)	amount: *total amount*	o total	too-**tahl**
all	todo(a), todos(as)	**toh**-doo(uh), **toh**-doosh(ush)	and	e	ee
allergic	alérgico(a)	a**lehr**-zheeko(uh)	angry	zangado(a)	zuñ**gahdoo**(uh)
I'm allergic to	sou alérgico(a)	soh a**lehr**-zheeko(uh)	animal	um animal	ooñ aneemahl
			to announce	anunciar	anoonsee**ar**
to allow	permitir	pehr-meeteer	another	um(a) outro(a)	ooñ **oh**-troo(truh)
to be allowed	estar permitido	eshtar pehr-meeteedoo	answer n	a resposta	resh-**posh**tuh
			to answer	responder	resh-pon**dehr**
all right	está bem	shta bayñ	antibiotic	o antibiótico	uñteebeee**oh**-teekoo
are you all right?	você está bem?	voh-**say** shta bayñ?	antihistamine	o anti-histamínico	uñtee-eestuh-**mee**neekoo
almost	quase	**kwah**-zuh			

English – Portuguese

English - Portuguese

English	Portuguese	Pronunciation	English	Portuguese	Pronunciation
anti-inflammatory	o anti-inflamatório	uñtee-eeñfluh-muh-**tor**yoo	arm	o braço	**brah**-soo
antiseptic	o antiséptico	uñteesep-teekoo	arrival	a chegada	shuh-**gah**-duh
any (some)	algum(a)	al**gooñ**/algoomuh	to arrive	chegar	shuh-**gar**
(negative)	nenhum(a)	nayn-**ooñ**/nayn-**yoom**uh	to ask (question)	perguntar	pehr-goon**tar**
anyone (in questions)	alguém	al**gayñ**	(to ask for something)	pedir	ped**eer**
(negative)	ninguém	neeñ**gayñ**	aspirin	a aspirina	ashpeereen**ash**
anything (in questions)	alguma coisa	algoomuh **koy**-zuh	asthma	a asma	**ash**muh
(negative)	nada	**nah**-duh	I have asthma	tenho asma	**ten**-yoo **ash**muh
apartment	o apartamento	uh-partuh-**meñt**oo	at	em; a	ayñ; uh
			at 8 o'clock	às oito	ash **oy**too
apple	a maçã	muh-**sañ**	at night	à noite	a noyt
appointment (meeting)	o encontro	ayñ-**koñt**roo	ATM	Multibanco®	mooltee-**buñk**oo
(doctor)	a consulta	koñsooltuh	attractive (person)	atraente	atrah-**eñt**
approximately	aproximada-mente	aprossee-mah-duh-**meñt**	automatic	automático(a)	owtomah-teekoo(uh)
			available	disponível	deesh-poh-**nee**-vel
			to avoid	evitar	eh-**veet**ar
			awful	terrível	teh-**rree**vel

English	Portuguese	Pronunciation
B		
baby	o bebé	be-be
baby's bottle	o biberão	bee-bayrowñ
baby seat (in car)	o assento do bebé	aseñtoo doo be-be
back (of body)	as costas	ush cosh-tush
bad (weather, news) (fruit, vegetables)	má (mau) podre	mah (mow) podruh
bag (case)	o saco a mala	sah-koo mah-luh
baggage	a bagagem	buh-gah-zhayñ
ball	a bola	boh-luh
bank	o banco	buñkoo
bank account	a conta bancária	koñtuh buñkar-yuh
bar	o bar	bar
barbecue	o churrasco	shoorrashkoo
basement	a cave	kahv
bath	o banho	bun-yoo
bathroom	a casa de banho	kah-zuh duh bun-yoo
battery (for car) (torch, radio, etc)	a bateria a pilha	batuh-ree-uh peelyuh
B&B	o quarto com pequeno-almoço oo	kwartoo koñ puh-kaynoo-almoh-soo
(place)	a pensão	payñ-sowñ
to be	ser; estar	sehr; esh-tar
beach	a praia	pry-uh
beautiful	belo(a); lindo(a)	beh-lo(uh); leeñdoo(uh)
because	porque	poorkuh
to become	tornar-se	tornar-suh
bed	a cama	kah-muh
bedroom	o quarto	kwartoo
beef	a carne de vaca; a vitela	karnduh vah-kuh; uh veetehluh
beer	a cerveja	servay-zhuh
before	antes (de)	uñtsh (duh)
to begin	começar	koomesar
behind	atrás (de)	uh-truz (duh)
to believe	acreditar	uh-krehdeetar

English - Portuguese

English	Portuguese	Pronunciation
to belong to	pertencer a	pehrtaÿ**sehr** a
below (less than)	abaixo (de)	a**by**shoo (duh)
beside (next to)	ao lado (de)	ow **lah**-doo (duh)
best: the best	o/a melhor	mel-**yor**
better (than)	melhor (do que)	mel-**yor** (doo kuh)
between	entre	**ayñ**truh
to beware of	ter cuidado	tehr **kweedah**-doo
bicycle	a bicicleta	beeseek**klay**tuh
big	grande	gruñd
bigger (than)	maior que	ma**yor** kuh
bill (in hotel, restaurant)	a conta	a **koñ**tuh
bill (for work done) (gas, telephone)	a factura	fa**too**ruh
	a conta	a **koñ**tuh
birthday	o aniversário	aneeversa**rÿoo**
happy birthday	parabéns	paruh-**bayñsh**
biscuits	as bolachas	ush boolashush
bit: a bit (of)	um bocado (de)	ooñ boo**kah**doo (duh)

English	Portuguese	Pronunciation
to bite (animal)	morder	moor**dehr**
(insect)	picar	peekar
bitten (by animal)	mordido(a)	moordee**doo**(uh)
(by insect)	picado(a)	peekahdoo
black	preto(a)	**preh**-too(uh)
to bleed	sangrar	suñ-**grar**
blind (person)	cego(a)	**seh**-goo(uh)
blond (person)	louro(a)	**low**-roo(uh)
blood	o sangue	**suñg**
blood pressure	a tensão arterial	tayñ-sowñ arterh-**yahl**
blood test	a análise ao sangue	unah-leezee ow **suñg**
blouse	a blusa	**bloo**zuh
blue	azul	a**zool**
to board (plane, train, etc)	embarcar	aÿñbar**kar**
boat	barco	**bar**koo
boarding card	o cartão de embarque	kartowñ duh ayñ-**bark**
body	o corpo	**kor**poo

English – Portuguese

English	Portuguese	Pronunciation
book	o livro	**lee**vroo
to book	reservar	ruh-zer**var**
booking	a reserva	ruh-**zehr**vuh
booking office	a bilheteria	beel-yeteh-**ree**-uh
bookshop	a livraria	leevruh-**ree**-uh
boots	as botas	ush **boh**tush
bottle	a garrafa	garrah-fuh
box	a caixa	**ky**-shuh
boy	o rapaz	ruh-**paysh**
boyfriend	o namorado	namoo-**rah**-doo
brandy	o conhaque	koon-**yah**kee
bread	o pão	powñ
to break	quebrar	ke**brar**
breakfast	o pequeno-almoço	puh-**kay**noo-almoh-soo
to breathe	respirar	resh-pee**rar**
bride	a noiva	**noy**vuh
bridegroom	o noivo	**noy**voo
bridge	a ponte	poñt
to bring	trazer	tra**zehr**
Britain	a Grã-Bretanha	grañ-bruh-**tun**-yuh
British	británico(a)	breetu**nee**koo
broken	partido(a)	par**tee**doo(uh)
broken down (car, etc)	avariado(a)	avaree-**ah**-doo
bronchitis	a bronquite	broñ**keet**
brother	o irmão	eer**mowñ**
brown	castanho(a)	kash-**tun**-yoo(uh)
to build	construir	koñsh-**tun**-troo-eer
bull	o touro	**toh**-roo
bullfight	a tourada	toh-**rah**-duh
bureau de change	a casa de câmbio	**kah**-zuh duh **kuñ**byoo
burger	um hambúrguer	uñ**boor**gehr
to burn	queimar	kay**mar**
bus	o autocarro	owtoo-**karro**o
bus pass	o passe de autocarro	pass duh owtoo-**karro**o

English – Portuguese

English	Portuguese	Pronunciation
bus station	a estação de autocarros	shtuh-**sowñ** duh owtoo-**karroo**
bus stop	a paragem de autocarros	parah-zhayñ duh owtoo-**karroo**
bus ticket	o bilhete de autocarro	beel-**yet** duh owtoo-**karroo**
business	os negócios	oosh negoh-seeoosh
on business	de negócios	duh negoh-seeoosh
business class	a classe executiva	klass ezeh-kooteevuh
busy	ocupado(a)	okoopah-doo/uh
but	mas	mush
butter	a manteiga	muñtay-guh
to buy	comprar	koñprar
by	por	poor
(near)	perto (de)	**pehr**-too (duh)
(next to)	ao lado (de)	ow **lah**-doo (duh)

by bus	de autocarro	duh owtoo-**karroo**
by train	de comboio	duh koñ**boy**oo
C		
café	o café	kuh-**fe**
cake	o bolo	**boh**-loo
cake shop	a pastelaria	pash-teluh-**ree**-uh
to call (telephone)	chamar	shuh-**mar**
call	uma chamada	**oo**muh shuh-**mah**-duh
camcorder	a camcorder	kuñ**kordehr**
camera	a máquina fotográfica	**make**enuh fotograh-feekuh
to camp	acampar	uh-kuñ**par**
campsite	o parque de campismo	park duh kuñ**peesh**-moo
can (to be able)	poder	poo**dehr**
Canada	o Canadá	kuh-nuh-**dah**

English	Portuguese	Pronunciation	English	Portuguese	Pronunciation
Canadian	canadiano(a)	kuh-nuh-dyuh-noo(uh)	to cash (cheque)	levantar	leh-vuñtar
to cancel	cancelar	kuñsuh-lar	cash desk	a caixa	ky-shuh
cancellation	o cancelamento	kuñsuhluh-meñtoo	cash machine	a caixa automática	ky-shuh owtoo-mah-teekuh
car	o carro	karroo	castle	o castelo	kush-teloo
car hire	o aluguer de automóveis	aloogehr duh owtoo-mohvaysh	casualty department	o Serviço de Urgências	sehr-vee-soo duh oor-zhayñ-see-ush
car insurance	o seguro de automóveis	segooroo duh owtoo-mohvaysh	cat	o gato	gah-too
			to catch (bus, train, etc)	apanhar	apun-yar
car park	o estacionamento	esh-tassyoonuh-meñtoo	cathedral	a catedral	kuh-tuh-drahl
caravan	a caravana	karuh-vunun	CD	o disco	deesh-koo
careful	cuidadoso(a)	kweeduh-dozoo	compacto	koñpaktoo	
be careful!	cuidado!	kwee**dah**-doo!	centimetre	o centímetro	sayñ-tee-metmetroo
to carry	transportar	truñspoor-tar	central	central	sayñ-trahl
case (suitcase)	a mala	mah-luh	central heating	o aquecimento central	akuh-seemeñtoo sayñ-trahl
cash	o dinheiro	deen-yay-roo	cent	o cêntimo	sayñ-tee-moo

English – Portuguese

English	Portuguese	Pronunciation
centre	o centro	**señ**troo
cereal (breakfast)	os cereais	oosh suh-reh-**ysh**
chair	a cadeira	kuh-**day**-ruh
champagne	o champanhe	shuñpuñ-yuh
change (coins)	o dinheiro	deen-**yay**-roo
	trocado	troo**kah**-doo
(money returned)	o troco	**troh**-koo
to change	trocar;	troo**kar**;
	mudar	moo**dar**
to change	trocar dinheiro	troo**kar** deen-
money		**yay**-roo
to change	mudar de roupa	moo**dar** duh
(clothes)		**roh**-puh
to change (train)	mudar	moo**dar**
changing room	o gabinete de	gubee-**net**
	provas	duh **proh**-vush
charge	o custo	**koosh**-too
cover charge	o couvert	koo**vehr**
to charge	cobrar	ko**brar**
cheap	barato(a)	barah-too(uh)
to check	verificar	veh-ree-fee**kar**
to check in (at airport)	fazer o check-in	fa**zehr** oo check-in
(at hotel)	apresentar-se	uh-preh-zañ-**tar**-suh
check-in desk	o balcão do	bal**kowñ** doo
	check-in	check-in
cheers!	saúde!	sah-**ood**!
cheese	o queijo	**kay**-zhoo
chef	o cozinheiro-chefe/	koo-zeen-**yay**roo shef/
	a cozinheira-chefe	koo-zeen-**yay**ruh shef
chemist's	a farmácia	far**mass**-yuh
chicken	a galinha;	ga**leen**-yuh;
	o frango	oo **fruñ**goo
child	a criança	kree-**uñ**suh
children	as crianças	ush kree-**uñ**sush
chilli	a malagueta	maluh-**getuh**
chips	as batatas fritas	ush **butah**-tush **free**-tush
chocolate	o chocolate	shoo-koo**laht**

English	Portuguese	Pronunciation
to choose	escolher	eesh-kohl-**yer**
Christmas	o Natal	nuh-**tahl**
church	a igreja	eegrehzbuh
cigarette	o cigarro	see-**gah**-rroo
cinema	o cinema	seeneh-muh
city	a cidade	seedahd
city centre	o centro (da cidade)	señtroo (duh seedahd)
class: first class	primeira classe	preemay/ruh klass
second class	segunda classe	suhgoon-duh klass
clean	limpo(a)	leeñpoo(uh)
to clean	limpar	leeñpar
client	o/a cliente	klee-**eñt**
to climb	subir	soo-**beer**
clock	o relógio	ruh-**lozh**-yoo
to close	fechar	fuh-**shar**
closed	fechado(a)	fuh-**shah**-doo(uh)
clothes	as roupas	ush roh-push
clothes shop	a loja de roupa	lozhuh duh roh-puh
cloudy	nublado(a)	nooblah-doo(uh)
coach	a camioneta	kuh-mee-oh-**neh**-tuh
coach station	a rodoviária	rodovear-yuh
coast	a costa	**kosh**-tuh
coat	o casaco	kuh-**zah**-koo
cod	o bacalhau	bah-kal-**yow**
coffee	o café	kuh-**fe**
coin	a moeda	**mway**-duh
cold	frio(a)	**free**-oo(uh)
it's cold	está frio	shta **free**-oo(uh)
cold (illness)	a constipação;	koñ-steepuh-**sowñ**,
to collect	colecionar	kolessyonar
to collect (to collect someone)	ir buscar	eer boosh-**kar**
colour	a cor	**kor**
to come (arrive)	vir	veer
	chegar	shuhgar
to come back	voltar	voltar
to come in	entrar	ayñtrar
come in!	entre!	ayñ-tree!

English – Portuguese

English	Portuguese	Pronunciation
comfortable	confortável	koñfortah-vel
company (firm)	a companhia	koñpun-yee-uh
to complain	queixar-se (de)	kay-shar-suh (duh)
complaint	uma queixa	oomuh kay-shuh
complete	completo(a)	koñpleh-too(uh)
to complete	completar	koñplaytar
computer	o computador	koñpootuh-dor
concert	o concerto	koñsehr-too
concession	o desconto	deeshkoñtoo
condom	o preservativo	prehzervuh-tee/voo
conference	a conferência	koñféh-rayñ-syuh
to confirm	confirmar	koñfeermar
confirmation (of booking)	a confirmação	koñfeermuh-sowñ
congratulations!	parabéns!	paruh-baynsh!
connection (flight, etc)	a ligação	lee-guh-sowñ
consulate	o consulado	koñsoolah-doo
to consult	consultar	koñsooltar
to contact	pôr-se em contacto com	por se ayñ koñtaktoo koñ
contact lenses	as lentes de contacto	ush leñtsh duh koñtaktoo
to continue	continuar	koñteenwar
contraception	a anticoncepção	uñteekoñsep-sowñ
convenient: is it convenient?	é conveniente?	e koñveh-nee-eñt?
to cook	cozinhar	kozeen-yar
cool	fresco(a)	fresh-koo(uh)
to copy	copiar	koopear
corner	o canto	kuñtoo
corridor	o corredor	koo-rredor
to cost	custar	kooshtar
cot	o berço	behr-soo
to cough	tossir	too-seer
cough	a tosse	toss
country	o país	pah-eesh
countryside	o campo	kuñpoo
couple (2 people)	o casal	kuh-zahl

English	Portuguese	Pronunciation
a couple of...	um par de	ooñ par duh
course (of meal)	o prato	**prah**-too
(of study)	o curso	**koor**-soo
cover charge	o couvert	koo-**vehr**
crash (car)	o choque	shok
cream (face, etc)	colidir	kolee-**deer**
(on milk)	o crème	krem
credit card	a nata	**nah**-tuh
	o cartão de	ka**towñ** duh
	crédito	**kred**eetoo
crime	o crime	**kree**muh
crisps	as batatinhas	ush butuh-**teen**-
	fritas	yush **free**tush
to cross (road)	cruzar	kroo**zar**
crossroads	o cruzamento	kroozuh-**meñ**too
crowded	cheio(a) de gente	**shay**oo(uh) duh
		zheñt
to cry (weep)	chorar	shoo**rar**
cucumber	o pepino	pee**pee**noo
cup	a chávena	**shah**-veh-nuh
currency	a moeda	**mway**-duh

English	Portuguese	Pronunciation
customer	o freguês/ a freguesa	fre**gaysh**/ uh fre**gayz**uh
customs (at airport etc)	a alfândega	al**fuñ**duh-guh
customs declaration	a declaração alfandegária	deh-klaruh-**sowñ** alfuñduh-**gar**-yuh
to cut	cortar	kor**tar**
cut	o corte	kort
cut and blow-dry	cortar e secar	kor**tar** ee seh-**kar**

D

English	Portuguese	Pronunciation
daily	cada dia	**kah**-duh **dee**-uh
dairy produce	os lacticínios	oosh lah-tee-**see**-nee-oosh
damage	os danos	oosh **dah**-noosh
danger	o perigo	peh-**ree**goo
dangerous	perigoso(a)	peh-**rego**zoo(uh)
dark adj	o escuro	esh-**koo**-roo
	escuro	esh-**koo**-roo

English – Portuguese

English – Portuguese

date	a data	**dah**-tuh	to depart	partir	par**teer**
date of birth	a data de nascimento	**dah**-tuh duh nashee-**men**too	departure lounge	a sala de embarque	**sah**-luh duh ayñ-**bark** ush par-**tee**-dush
daughter	a filha	**feel**-yuh	departures	as partidas	
day	o dia	**dee**-uh	deposit	o depósito	duh-**po**zeetoo
every day	todos os dias	**toh**-doosh oosh **dee**-ush	to describe	descrever	desh-kreh-**vehr**
			desk (in hotel, airport)	a secretária	suh-kreh-**tar**-yuh
per day	por dia	poor **dee**-uh	dessert	o balcão	balko**wñ**
deaf	surdo(a)	**soor**-doo(uh)	details	a sobremesa	sobruh-**may**-zuh oosh poor-meh-
death	a morte	mort		os pormenores	**nor**-ush
debt	a dívida	**dee**-veeduh	to develop (person)	desenvolver	dezeñvol**vehr**
to declare: nothing to declare	nada a declarar	**nah**-duh uh deklara**r**	diabetic (person)	diabético(a)	dee-uh-**bet**eekoo(kuh)
deep	fundo(a)	**fun**-doo(uh)	to dial	marcar	mar**kar**
delay	a demora	deh-**mor**-uh	dialling code	o código	**ko**deegoo
delayed	atrasado(a)	atruh-**zah**-doo(uh)	to die	morrer	moo-**rrehr**
			diesel	o gasóleo	ga**zol**-yoo
dentist	o/a dentista	deñ**teesh**tuh	diet	a dieta	dee-**ehtuh**
deodorant	o desodorizante	deh-zodoree-**zuñt**	I'm on a diet	estou de dieta	shto duh dee-**ehtuh**

English	Portuguese	Pronunciation	English	Portuguese	Pronunciation
different	diferente	dee-fer**eñt**	to discover	descobrir	deeshkoo**breer**
difficult	difícil	deefee-seel	disease	a doença	doo-**eñ**suh
digital camera	a câmara digital	**kum**ah-ruh deezhee-**tahl**	distance	a distância	deesh-**tuñss**-yuh
dining room	a sala de jantar	**sah**-luh duh zhuñ**tar**	to disturb	incomodar	eeñkomo**dar**
dinner	o jantar	zhuñ**tar**	diversion	o desvio	deesh-**vee**-oo
direct	directo(a)	dee**rekt**o(uh)	divorced	divorciado(a)	devoors-**yah**-doo(uh)
directions (instructions)	instruções	eeñstroos-**oyñsh**	dizzy	tonto(a)	**toñ**-too(uh)
directory (phone)	a lista telefónica	**leesh**tuh tuh-luh-**fon**eekuh	to do	fazer	fa**zehr**
			doctor	o/a médico(a)	**med**eeko(uh)
dirty	sujo(a)	**soo**-zhoo(uh)	documents	os documentos	dokoo**meñ**toosh
disabled	deficiente	duh-feess-**yeñt**	dog (male)	o cão	**kowñ**
disabled person	o/a deficiente	duh-feess-**yeñt**	(female)	a cadela	kuh-**deh**-luh
to disagree	discordar	deesh-kor**dar**	dollar	o dólar	**dol**ur
to disappear	desaparecer	dezuh-pa**ressehr**	door	a porta	**port**uh
disappointed	desiludido(a)	dee-zee-loo-**dee**-doo(uh)	double	o dobro	**dob**roo
disco	a discoteca	deesh-ko**teh**-kuh	double bed	a cama de casal	**kah**-muh duh kuh-**zahl**
discount	o desconto	deesh**koñ**too	double room	o quarto de casal	**kwar**too duh kuh-**zahl**

English	Portuguese	Pronunciation
down: to go down	descer	desh-**sehr**
draught (of air)	a corrente de ar	koo-**rreñt**duh ar
draught lager	a imperial	eeñpehr-**yahl**
dress	o vestido	veesh-**teedoo**
to dress (oneself)	vestir-se	veesh-**teer**-suh
dressing (for food)	o tempero; o molho	tayñ**peroo**; oo **mol**-yoo
(for wound)	o penso	oo **payñ**-soo
drink	a bebida	beh-**bee**-duh
to drink	beber	beh-**behr**
drinking water	a água potável	**ahg**-wuh pootah-vel
to drive	conduzir	koñdoo**zeer**
driver	o/a condutor(a)	koñdootor(uh)
driving licence	a carta de condução	kartuh duh koñdoo**sowñ**
to drown	afogar	afoo-**gar**
drug (medicine)	o medicamento	medeekuh-**meñtoo**
(narcotic)	a droga	**drog**uh
drunk	bêbedo(a)	**bay**-beh-doo(uh)
dry	seco(a)	**seh**-koo(uh)
to dry	secar	seh-**kar**
dryer	o secador	seh-kuh-**dor**
during	durante	dooruñt
duty (tax)	o imposto	eeñ**posh**-too
duty-free	livre de impostos	**lee**-vree duh eeñ**posh**-toosh

E

English	Portuguese	Pronunciation
each	cada	**kah**-duh
ear	a orelha	oo-**rel**-yuh
earache	a dor de ouvidos	dor duh oh-**vee**doosh
early	cedo	**seh**-doo
east	o leste	laysht
Easter	a Páscoa	**pash**-koo-uh
easy	fácil	**fah**-seel
to eat	comer	ko**mehr**
egg	o ovo	**oh**-voo
Elastoplast®	o penso	**payñ**-soo

English	Portuguese	Pronunciation
electric	eléctrico(a)	eléktreekoo(uh)
electric razor	a máquina de barbear	makeenuh duh barbee-**ar**
e-mail	o correio electrónico;	koorrayoo eletroh-neekoo;
embarrassing	embaraçoso(a)	ayñ-barruh-**sozoo**(uh)
embassy	a embaixada	ayñby-**shah**-duh
emergency	a emergência	emehr-**zhayñ**-syuh
emergency exit	a saída de emergência	sah-**eeduh** duh emehr-**zhayñ**-syuh
empty	vazio(a)	vuh-**zee**-oo(uh)
end	o fim	feeñ
engaged	comprometido(a)	koñpro-meh-**tee**-doo(uh)
(phone, toilet, etc)	ocupado(a)	oko-**pah**-doo(uh)
England	a Inglaterra	eeñ-gluh-**terr**-uh
English	inglês (inglesa)	eeñ**glaysh** (eeñ**glayzuh**)
(language)	o inglês	o eeñ**glaysh**
enjoy oneself	divertir-se	deevehrteer-suh
enormous	enorme	eh-**norm**
enough	bastante	bush**tuñt**
that's enough	chega	**sheh**-guh
enquiries	as informações	ush eeñfoormuh-**soyñsh**
enquiry desk	o balcão de informações	balkowñ duh eeñfoormuh-**soyñsh**
to enter	entrar (em)	ayñ-**trar** (ayñ)
enthusiastic	entusiástico(a)	ayñ-too-zee-**ash**-tee-koo(uh)
entrance	a entrada	eñ**trah**-duh
entrance fee	o bilhete de entrada	beel-**yet** duh eñ**trah**-duh
error	o erro	**err**-oo
escalator	a escada rolante	eshkah-duh rol**uñt**
estate agent	a imobiliária	eemoo-bee-lee-**ar**-yuh

English – Portuguese

English – Portuguese

English	Portuguese	
euro	o euro	eoo-roo
Europe	a Europa	ayoo-**roh**-puh
European	europeu (européia)	ayoo-roo**peh**-oo (ayoo-roo**peh**-yuh)
eve	a véspera	**vesh**-peruh
evening	a noite	noyt
every	cada	**kah**-duh
everyone	toda a gente; todos	**toh**-duh uh zheñt; **toh**-doosh
everything	todas as coisas; tudo	**toh**-dush ush **koy**-zush; **too**doo
everywhere	por todo o lado	poor **toh**-doo oo **lah**-doo
example: for example	por exemplo	poor eh-**zayñ**-ploo
excellent	excelente	esh-se**leñt**
except	excepto	es-**sep**too
excess baggage /luggage	o excesso de bagagem	es **seh**-soo duh buh-**gah**-zhayñ
to exchange	trocar	troo**kar**
exchange rate	o câmbio	**kuñ**bee-oo
exciting	emocionante	emoh-syonu**ñt**
excuse	a desculpa	dush-**koolp**
exercise (physical)	o exercício	e-zehr-**see**-syoo
exit	a saída	sah-**ee**duh
expenses	as despesas	desh-**peh**-zush
expensive	caro(a)	**kah**-roo(uh)
expiry date	o vencimento	vayñ-see-**meñt**oo
to explain	explicar	eesh-plee**kar**
extra	extra	**es**-truh
eye	o olho	**ohl**-yoo
F		
facilities	as instalações	eeñstaluhso**yñsh**
to fail	fracassar	fruh-kuh-**sar**
(engine, brakes)	falhar	fal-**yar**
to faint	desmaiar	deesh-my-**ar**

English	Portuguese	Pronunciation
fair (hair)	louro(a)	loh-roo(uh)
(just)	justo(a)	zhoosh-too(uh)
fake	falso(a)	fahl-soo(uh)
to fall	cair	kah-eer
he/she has fallen	ele/ela caiu	ayl/ayluh kuh-yoo
family	a família	fuh-meel-yuh
famous	famoso(a)	fuh-mozoo(uh)
far	longe	lõzh
is it far?	é longe?	e lõzh?
how far is it to...?	a que distância fica...?	kuh deesh-tuñss-yuh fee-kuh?
fare (train, bus, etc)	(da passagem)	pray-soo (duh puh-sah-zhayñ)
	o preço	
fast	rápido(a)	rah-peedoo(uh)
too fast	rápido(a) demais	rah-peedoo(uh) duh-mysh
to fasten (seatbelt)	apertar	apehr-tar
fat	gordo(a)	gor-doo(uh)
father	o pai	py
fault (defect)	o defeito	duh-fay-too
favour	o favor	fuh-vor
favourite	favorito(a)	fuh-vooreetoo(uh)
fax	o fax	faks
by fax	por fax	poor faks
to feel	sentir	sayñ-teer
I feel sick	tenho náuseas	ten-yoo now-zee-ush
I don't feel well	sinto-me mal-disposto(a)	seeñ-too-muh mahl-deesh-posh-too(uh)
feet	os pés	pesh
female	a mulher	mool-yehr
to fetch (to go and get)	ir buscar	eer boosh-kar
fever	a febre	februh
few	poucos(as)	pohkoosh(ush)
a few	alguns (algumas)	algooñ (algoomush)
fiancé(e)	o/a noivo(a)	noyvoo(uh)
fight	a briga	breeguh
to fight	brigar	breegar

English – Portuguese

English – Portuguese

English	Portuguese	Pronunciation
to fill	encher	ayñ-**shehr**
fill it up!	encha o depósito!	**ayñ**-shuh oo duh-**pozee**too!
to fill in (form)	preencher	prayñ-**shehr**
fillet	o filete	feelmuh
film (at cinema)	o filme	feelmuh
(for camera)	o rolo de filme	roloo duh feelmuh
to find	achar	ashar
fine (to be paid)	a multa	mooltuh
to finish	acabar	akuh-**bar**
finished	acabado(a)	akuh-**bah**-doo(uh)
fire	o fogo	fogoo
fire alarm	o alarme de incêndios	alarm duh eeñsayñ-dyoosh
fire escape	a saída de incêndios	sah-**ee**duh duh eeñsayñ-dyoosh
fire extinguisher	o extintor	esh-teeñ**tor**
firm (company)	a firma	feermuh
first	o/a primeiro(a)	preemay-roo(uh)

English	Portuguese	Pronunciation
first aid	os primeiros socorros	preemay-roosh sookorroosh
first class	a primeira classe	preemay-ruh klass
first name	o nome próprio	nom **prop**ree-oo
fish	o peixe	paysh
to fish	pescar	peshkar
to fit: *it doesn't fit me*	não me serve	nowñ muh serv
fit	o ataque	uh-**takuh**
to fix	reparar	repuh-**rar**
fizzy	gasoso(a)	gazozoo(uh)
flat (apartment)	o apartamento	uh-partuh-**meñtoo**
flat (battery)	plano(a) descarregado	**pluh**-noo(uh) desh-karruh-**gah**-doo
flavour	o sabor	suh-**bor**
flight	o voo	**voh**-oo
floor (storey)	o chão	**showñ**
	o andar	uñ**dar**

English	Portuguese	
ground floor	o rés-do-chão	resh-doo-**showñ**
first floor	o primeiro andar	preemay-roo uñ**dar**
flower	a flor	flor
flu	a gripe	greep
to fly	voar	vooar
fog	o nevoeiro	nuhvooayroo
foggy	nevoento	nuhvooayñtoo
food	a comida	koomeeduh
food poisoning	a intoxicação alimentar	eeñtokseekuh-**sowñ** aleemeñ**tar**
foot	o pé	pe
on foot	a pé	pe
football	o futebol	footbol
for	para	paruh
for me	para mim	paruh meeñ
forbidden	proibido(a)	proee-**bee**doo
forecast	a previsão	preeve**zowñ**
weather forecast	a previsão do tempo	preeve**zowñ** doo **tayñ**poo

English	Portuguese	
foreign	estrangeiro(a)	eesh-truñ-**zhay**-roo(uh)
foreigner	o/a estrangeiro(a)	eesh-truñ-**zhay**-roo(uh)
forever	para sempre	paruh **sayñ**ruh
to forget	esquecer-se de	eesh-kuh-**ser**-suh duh
fork (for eating)	o garfo	**gar**foo
(in road)	a bifurcação	bee-foorkuh-**sowñ**
form (document)	o formulário	formoo-**lar**yoo
fracture	a fractura	fruktooruh
fragile	frágil	**frah**-zheel
free (not occupied)	livre	**lee**-vree
(costing nothing)	grátis	**grah**-teesh
freezer	o congelador	koñzhuh-luh-**dor**
frequent	frequente	fruh-**kweñt**
fresh	fresco(a)	**fresh**-koo(uh)
Friday	a sexta-feira	seshtuh-**fay**ruh
fried	frito(a)	**free**too(uh)
friend	o/a amigo(a)	uh-**mee**goo(uh)

English – Portuguese

English – Portuguese

English	Portuguese	Pronunciation
friendly	simpático(a)	see**pah**-teekoo(uh) duh
from	de	duh
from England	da Inglaterra	duh eeñ-gluh-**terr**-uh
front	a frente	freñt
in front of	em frente de	ayñ freñt duh
fruit	a fruta	**froo**tuh
to fry	fritar	freetar
fuel (petrol)	a gasolina	gazoolee-nuh
full	cheio(a)	**shay**oo(uh)
full board	a pensão completa	payñ-**sowñ** koñ**pleh**-tuh
fun	a diversão	deevehr-**sowñ**
funny	engraçado(a)	eeñgryuh-**sah**doo(uh)
(strange)	estranho(a)	eestrun-yoo(uh)
furnished	mobilado(a)	moobeelah-doo
furniture	a mobília	moobeel-yuh

G

English	Portuguese	Pronunciation
gallery (art)	a galeria de arte	galeh-**ree**-uh duh art
game	o jogo	**zhoh**-goo
garage (private)	a garagem	guh-**rah**-zheñ
(for repairs)	a oficina (de reparos)	oofee-**see**nuh (duh reh**pah**-roosh)
(for petrol)	a estação de serviço	shta**sowñ** duh servee-soo
garden	o jardim	zhar**deeñ**
gas	o gás	gahs
generous	generoso(a)	zheneroo-zoo(uh)
gents' (toilet)	Homens	**om**ayñsh
genuine (leather, antique etc)	autêntico(a)	owtayñ-teekoo (uh)
to get (to obtain)	obter	ob**tehr**
(to receive)	receber	ruh-seh-**behr**
(to fetch)	ir buscar	eer booshkar
to get in (vehicle)	subir em	soo**beer** ayñ
to get into	entrar em	ayñ-**trar** ayñ

English	Portuguese	Pronunciation
to get off	descer de	desh-**sehr** duh
to get on (vehicle)	subir para	soo**beer** paruh
gift	o presente;	pruh-**zeñt**;
	a prenda	uh **prayn**-duh
gift shop	a loja de	**lozhuh** duh
	lembranças	layñ-**bruñ**-sush
girl	a rapariga	ruh-pareeguh
girlfriend	a namorada	namoo**rah**-duh
to give	dar	dar
to give back	devolver	duh-vol**vehr**
glass (substance)	o vidro;	**veed**roo;
	o cristal	creesh-**tahl**
(to drink out of)	o copo	**kopo**o
glasses	os óculos	oosh **oh**-kooloosh
to go	ir	eer
I'm going to...	vou para...	voh pa**ruh**...
we're going to...	vamos para...	**vuh**-moosh paruh...
to go back	voltar	vol**tar**
to go down	descer	desh-**sehr**
to go in	entrar (em)	ayñ-**trar** (ayñ)

English	Portuguese	Pronunciation
to go out	saír	sah-**eer**
good	bom (boa)	boñ (**boh**-uh)
very good	muito bom	**mween**to boñ
gram	o grama	**gruh**-muh
grandchild	o/a neto(a)	**neh**-too(uh)
grandparents	os avós	oosh uh-**vosh**
grapes	as uvas	ush **oo**vush
great (big)	grande	gruñd
(wonderful)	óptimo(a)	**otee**-moo(uh)
Great Britain	a Grã-Bretanha	grañ-bruh-**tun**-yuh
green	verde	verd
greengrocer's	a frutaria	frootuh-**ree**-uh
grocer's	a mercearia	mehrsee-uh-**ree**-uh
ground (earth)	a terra	**terr**-uh
(floor)	o chão	**showñ**
ground floor	o rés-do-chão	resh-doo-**showñ**
on the ground floor...	no rés-do-chão...	noo resh-doo-**showñ**...
group	o grupo	**groo**poo

English - Portuguese

English – Portuguese

guarantee	a garantia	guh-ruñ**tee**-uh
guest	o/a convidado(a)	koñvee**dah**-doo(uh)
(in hotel)	o/a hóspede	**osh**-peeduh
guesthouse	a pensão	payñ-**sowñ**
guide	o/a guia	**ghee**-uh
guidebook	a guia	**ghee**-uh
guided tour	a excursão guiada	eeshkoor**sowñ** ghee-**ah**-duh

H

hair	o cabelo	kuh-**bay**-loo
hairdresser	o/a cabeleireiro(a)	kuh-**bay**-lay-**ray**-roo(uh)
half	a metade	meh-**tahd**
a half bottle of	meia garrafa de	**may**uh garrah-fuh duh
half an hour	meia hora	**may**uh oruh
half board	a meia pensão	**may**uh payñ-**sowñ**
half fare	meio-bilhete	**may**oo beel-**yet**

half-price	pela metade do preço	peluh meh-**tahd** doo **pray**-soo
ham (boiled)	fiambre	fee-**uñ**-bruh
ham (smoked)	presunto	pruh-**zoon**too
hamburger	o hambúrguer	uñ**boor**gehr
hand	a mão	mowñ
handbag	a bolsa	**bol**suh
handicapped (person)	deficiente	duh-feess-**yeñt**
hand luggage	a bagagem de mão	buh-**gah**-zhayñ duh mowñ
hand-made	feito(a) à mão	**fay**too(uh) a mowñ
handsome	bonito(a); giro(a)	boonee**too**(uh); **zhee**roo(uh)
to hang up (phone)	desligar	deesh-leegar
to happen	acontecer	uh-koñte**sehr**
what happened?	o que aconteceu?	oo kuh uh-koñte**sayoo**?
happy	feliz	fuh-**leesh**

hard (difficult)	duro(a)	**doo**-roo(uh)
	difícil	deefee-seel
to have	ter	tehr
I (don't) have...	eu (não) tenho...	ay-oo (nowñ) **ten**-yoo...
we (don't) have...	nós (não)	nosh (nowñ)
	temos...	**tay**moosh...
do you have...?	tem...?	tayñ...?
to have to	ter que;	tehr kuh;
	ter de	tehr duh
hay fever	a febre dos	**feb**ruh doosh
	fenos	**feh**-noosh
he	ele	ayl
headache	a dor de cabeça	dor duh kuh-**beh**-suh
I have a headache	dói-me a cabeça	**doy**-muh uh kuh-**beh**-suh
health	a saúde	sah-**ood**
healthy	saudável	sow**dah**-vel
to hear	ouvir	oh-**veer**
heart	o coração	kooruh-**sowñ**

to heat up	aquecer	akuh-**sehr**
heavy	pesado(a)	peh-**zah**-doo(uh)
height	a altura	a**too**ruh
hello	olá	oh-**lah**
(on phone)	está?	shta?
help	a ajuda	uh-**zhoo**duh
help!	socorro!	soo**korro**o!
to help	ajudar	azhoo**dar**
can you help me?	pode-me ajudar?	**pod**-muh azhoo**dar?**
here	aqui	uh-**kee**
hi!	olá!	oh-**lah!**
to hide (something)	esconder	eeshkoñ**dehr**
(oneself)	esconder-se	eeshkoñ**dehr**-suh
high (price, speed, building)	alto(a)	**ahl**too(uh)
(number)	grande	gruñd
him (direct object)	o	oo
(indirect object)	lhe	lyuh
(after preposition)	ele	ayl

English – Portuguese

English – Portuguese

English	Portuguese	Pronunciation
hire	o aluguer	aloogehr
car hire	o aluguer de carros	aloogehr duh karroosh
to hire	alugar	aloogar
hobby	o passatempo	passuh-taynĩ-poo
to hold (to contain)	conter	koñtehr
holiday	as férias	fehr-yush
(public holiday)	o feriado	fuh-ree-ah-doo
on holiday	de férias	duh fehr-yush
home	a casa	kah-zuh
at home	em casa	ayñ kah-zuh
to go home	voltar para casa	voltar paruh kah-zuh
honeymoon	a lua-de-mel	loo-uh duh mel
to hope	esperar	eesh-peh-rar
I hope so/not	espero que sim/ não	eesh-peh-roo kuh seeñ/nowñ
hospital	o hospital	oshpeetahl
hot	quente	keñt
I'm hot	tenho calor	ten-yoo kalor
it's hot	está quente	shta keñt

English	Portuguese	Pronunciation
it's hot (weather)	faz/está calor	fash/shta kalor
hotel	o hotel	oh-tel
hour	a hora	oruh
half an hour	meia hora	mayuh oruh
1 hour	uma hora	oomuh oruh
2 hours	duas horas	doo-ush oruz
house	a casa	kah-zuh
how	como	koh-moo
how much?	quanto(a)?	kwuñĩtoo(uh)?
how many?	quantos(as)?	kwuñĩcoosh(ush)?
how are you?	como está?	koh-moo shta?
hundred	cem	sayñ
hungry: I am hungry	tenho fome	ten-yoo fom
hurry: I'm in a hurry	tenho pressa	ten-yoo preh-suh
to hurt	doer	doo-ehr
that hurts	isso dói	e-soo doy
husband	o marido	muhreedoo

I	eu	ay-oo	in London	em Londres	ayñ **loñ**drush
ice	o gelo	**zhay**-loo	in front of	em frente de	ayñ freñt duh
ice cream	o gelado	zhuh-**lah**-doo	inch	= approx. 2.5 cm	
ice lolly	o gelado; o picolé	zhuh-**lah**-doo; peekoh-**le**	included	incluído(a)	eeñkloo-**eedoo**(uh)
identity card	o bilhete de identidade	beel-**yet** duh edeñteе**dahd**	to increase	aumentar	owmeñ**tar**
if	se	suh	indigestion	a indigestão	eeñdee-zhesh-**towñ**
ill	doente	doo-**eñt**	infection	a infecção	eeñfek-**sowñ**
I'm ill	estou doente	shto doo-**eñt**	information	a informação	eeñfoormuh-**sowñ**
illness	a doença	doo-**ayñ**suh	to injure	lesionar	leh-zyo**nar**
immediately	imediatamente	eemuh-dee-ah-tuh-**meñt**	injured	ferido(a)	fuh-**reedoo**(uh)
important	importante	eeñpor**tuñt**	inquiries	as informações	eeñfoormuh-**soyñsh**
impossible	impossível	eeñpoo-**see**-vel	insect	o insecto	eeñ**señ**-too
to improve	melhorar	mel-yo**rar**	inside	dentro	**deñ**troo
in	em	ayñ	instead of	em vez de	ayñ vesh duh
(within)	dentro de	**deñ**troo duh	insurance	o seguro	se**goo**roo
in 10 minutes	dentro de dez minutos	**deñ**troo duh desh mee**noo**tosh	insurance certificate	a apólice de seguro	uh-**polee**see duh se**goo**roo

English – Portuguese

English – Portuguese

English	Portuguese	Pronunciation
insured: to be insured	estar no seguro	esh-**tar** noo segooroo
intelligent	inteligente	eeñteh-lee-**zheñt**
to intend to	tencionar fazer	tayñ-syonar fa**zehr**
interesting	interessante	eeñteh-reh-**ssuñt**
internet	a internet	eeñternet
international	internacional	eeñternasyo**nahl**
into	em; a; para	ayñ; uh; paruh
into the centre	ao centro	ow **señ**troo
invitation	o convite	koñ**veet**
to invite	convidar	koñvee**dar**
Ireland	a Irlanda	eerluñduh
Irish	irlandês (irlandesa)	eerluñ**daysh** (eerluñday-zuh)
iron (metal)	o ferro	**ferr**-oo duh
iron (for clothes)	o ferro de engomar	**ferr**-oo duh ayñgomar
island	a ilha	eel-yuh
to itch	fazer comichão	fa**zehr** komeesho**wñ**
it itches	faz comichão	fash komeesho**wñ**
J		
jacket	o casaco	kuh-**zah**-koo
jam	a compota	koñ**potuh**
jammed (stuck)	bloqueado(a)	bloh-kee-**ah**-doo(uh)
jar	o jarro	**zharroo**
jealous	ciumento(a)	syoo**meñ**too(uh)
jeans	as jeans	ush zheeñsh
jewel	a jóia	**zhoy**-uh
jewellery	a joalharia	zhwal-yuh-**ree**-uh
job	o emprego	ayñ-**preh**-goo
to join (club)	associar-se a	assosseear-suh
to join in	participar	partee-seepar
to joke	brincar	breeñkar
journalist	o/a jornalista	zhornaleeshtuh
journey	a viagem	vee-**ah**-zhayñ
juice	o sumo	**soo**moo
to jump	saltar	saltar

junction	o cruzamento	kroozuh-**meñ**too
just: just two	apenas dois	uh-**peh**-nush doysh
I've just arrived	acabo de chegar	uh-**kah**-boo duh shuh-**gar**

K

to keep (retain)	guardar	gwar**dar**
keep the change!	fique com o troco!	feek koñ oo **troko**!
key	a chave	shahv
to kill	matar	muh-**tar**
kilo	o quilo	**keeloo**
kilometre	o quilómetro	keelometroo
kind (person)	amável	uh-**mah**-vel
kind (sort)	a espécie	eeshpessee-uh
kiosk	o quiosque	**kee**-oshk
kiss	o beijo	**bay**-zhoo
to kiss	beijar	bay-**zhar**
kitchen	a cozinha	koozeen-yuh

to knock (on door)	bater	buh-**tehr**
to know (have knowledge of)	saber	suh-**behr**
to know (person, place)	conhecer	koon-yeh-**sehr**
I don't know	não sei	nowñ **say**
to know how to swim	saber nadar	suh-**behr** nuh-**dar**

L

lady	a senhora	sun-**yoru**
lager	a cerveja	servay-zhuh
bottled lager	a cerveja de garrafa	servay-zhuh duh garrah-fuh
draught lager	a imperial	eeñpehr-**yahl**
lamb	o cordeiro	koor-**day**-roo
to land	aterrar	aterrar
language	a língua	**leeñ**gwuh
large	grande	gruñd
last	último(a)	**oolt**eemoo(uh)
last night	ontem à noite	oñ-tayñ a noyt

English – Portuguese

English – Portuguese

last week	a semana passada	suh-**mah**-nuh puh-**sah**-duh
last year	o ano passado	**ah**-noo puh-**sah**-doo
the last time	a última vez	**oolt**eemuh vesh
late	tarde	tard
the train is late	o comboio está atrasado	koñ**boyo**o shta atruh-**zah**-doo
sorry we are late	desculpe o atraso	dushkoolp oo uh-**trah**-zoo
later	mais tarde	mysh tard
to laugh	rir	reer
lavatory	o lavabo	luh-**vah**-boo
law	a lei	lay
to learn	aprender	aprayñ-**dehr**
least: at least	pelo menos	**peh**-loo meh-noosh
leather	o couro	**koh**-roo
to leave (leave behind)	deixar	day-**shar**
(train, bus etc)	partir	par**teer**

when does it leave?	a que horas parte?	a kee **oruz** part?
left: on/to the left	à esquerda	a **shkehr**-duh
left luggage (office)	o depósito de bagagens	duh-**pozee**too duh-bah-**gah**-zhayñs
leg	a perna	**pehr**-nuh
lemonade	a limonada	leemo**nah**-duh
to lend	emprestar	aympresh-**tar**
length	o comprimento	koñpree**meñ**too
lenses (contact lenses)	as lentes de contacto	ush leñtsh duh koñ**tak**too
less	menos	**meh**-noosh
less than	menos do que	**meh**-noosh doo kuh
let (allow)	deixar	day-**shar**
(lease)	alugar	aloo**gar**
letter	a carta	**kar**tuh
(of alphabet)	a letra	**le**truh

English – Portuguese

English	Portuguese	Pronunciation
licence (driving)	a licença / a carta de condução	lee-**sayñ**-suh / **kar**tuh duh koñdoo**sowñ**
lie (untruth)	a mentira	meñ**teer**uh
life	a vida	**vee**-duh
lift (elevator)	o elevador	eeluh-vuh-**dor**
(in car)	a boleia	boo-**lay**-uh
light	a luz	loosh
light (not heavy)	leve	lev
(colour)	claro(a)	**klah**-roo(uh)
like	como	**koh**-moo
it's like this	é assim	e uh-**seeñ**
to like	gostar de	goosh**tar** duh
I (don't) like coffee	(não) gosto de café	(nowñ) **gosh**too duh kuh-**fe**
I'd like to...	gostava de...	goosh**tah**-vuh duh...
we'd like to...	gostávamos de...	goosh**tah**-vuh-moosh duh...
line (row, queue)	a fila	**feel**uh
(phone)	a linha	**leen**-yuh
list	a lista	**leesh**tuh
to listen to	ouvir	oh-**veer**
litre	o litro	**leet**roo
litter (rubbish)	o lixo	**lee**shoo
little	pequeno(a)	puh-**kay**noo(uh)...
a little...	um pouco de...	ooñ **poh**koduh...
to live	viver; morar	vee**vehr**; moo**rar**
local	local	lo**kahl**
to lock	fechar com chave	fuh-**shar** koñ shahv
locker (luggage)	o depósito de bagagem	duh-**poz**eetoo duh buh-**gah**-zhayñ
London	Londres	**loñ**drush
in London	em Londres	ayñ **loñ**drush
to London	a Londres	a **loñ**drush
long	comprido(a); longo(a)	koñ**preed**oo(uh); **loñ**goo(uh)

English - Portuguese

English	Portuguese	Pronunciation
for a long time	durante muito tempo	dooruñt mweeñto tayñ-poo
to look after	cuidar de	kwee-dar duh
to look at	olhar	ol-yar
to look for	procurar	prokoorar
to lose	perder	pehr-dehr
lost	perdido(a)	pehr-deedoo(uh)
I have lost my wallet	perdi a minha carteira	pehr-dee uh meen-yuh kar-tay-ruh
I am lost	estou perdido(a)	shto pehr-deedoo(a)
lost property office	a secção de perdidos e achados	uh seksowñ duh perdee-doosh ee uh-shah-doosh
lot: a lot (much) (many)	muito(a) muitos(as)	mweeñtoo(uh) mweeñtoosh (ush)

English	Portuguese	Pronunciation
loud (noisy) (volume)	ruidoso(a) alto(a)	rwee-dozoo(uh) ahltoo(uh)
lounge (in hotel, house)	a sala de estar	sah-luh duh esh-tar
(in airport)	o salão	salowñ
to love	amar	ah-mar
I love swimming	adoro nadar	uh-doroo nuh-dar
lovely	encantador(a)	eeñkuñtuh-dor(uh)
low	baixo(a)	byshoo(uh)
lucky: to be lucky	ter sorte	tehr sort
luggage	a bagagem	buh-gah-zhayñ
lunch	o almoço	almoh-soo
luxury	o luxo	loo-shoo

M

English	Portuguese	Pronunciation
machine	a máquina	makeenuh
madam	a senhora	sun-yoruh
magazine	a revista	ruveesh-tuh

maid	a empregada	eeñprе**grah**-duh
mail	o correio	koorrayoo
by mail	pelo correio	**peh**-loo koorrayoo
main	principal	preeñseepahl
main course (of meal)	o prato principal	**prah**-too preeñseepahl
main road	a estrada principal	eeñ**shtrah**-duh preeñseepahl
to make (generally)	fazer	fazehr
(meal)	preparar	preh-parar
make-up	a maquilhagem	muh-keel-**yah**-zhayñ
male	masculino(a)	mash-kooleenoo(uh)
man	o homem	omayñ
to manage (cope)	arranjar-se	arruñ**zhar**-suh
manager	o/a gerente	zhereñt
many	muitos(as)	**mween**toosh (ush)
map	o mapa	**mah**-puh

market	o mercado	merkah-doo
where is the market?	onde fica o mercado?	oñduh **feekuh** oo merkah-doo?
when is the market?	quando há mercado?	**kwuñ**doo a merkah-doo?
married	casado(a)	kuh-**zah**-doo(uh)
I'm married	sou casado(a)	soh kuh-**zah**-doo(uh)
are you married?	é casado(a)?	e kuh-**zah**-doo(uh)?
marry: to get married	casar(-se)	kuh-**zar**(-suh)
material (cloth)	o material	matehr-**yahl**
to matter: *it doesn't matter*	o tecido	teh-**see**doo
	não tem importância	nowñ tayñ eeñpoor**tuñss**-yuh
maximum	o máximo	**mah**-seemoo
meal	a refeição	ruhfay**sowñ**
to mean	significar	seeg-neefee**kar**

English – Portuguese

English – Portuguese

what does this mean?	o que quer dizer isto?	kee kehr deezehr **eesh**too?	
to measure	medir	meh-**deer**	
meat	a carne	karn	
I don't eat meat	não como carne	nowñ **koh**-moo karn	
medicine	o medicamento	medeekuh-**meñ**too	
medium	médio(a)	**med**-yoo(uh)	
medium rare (meat)	meio-passado(a)	**mayo**o puh-**sah**-doo(uh)	
to meet (by chance)	encontrar	ayñkoñ**trar**	
(by arrangement)	encontrar-se	ayñkoñ**trar**-suh	
	com	koñ	
pleased to meet you	prazer em conhecê-lo(a)	pruh-**zehr** ayñ koon-ye-**say**-loo(uh)	
memory (thing remembered)	a memória	meh-**mor**-yuh	
memory card	o cartão	kar**towñ**	

(for digital camera)	a memória	meh-**mor**-yuh	
men	os homens	**oh**mayñsh	
to mend	arranjar;	arruñ**zhar**;	
	consertar	koñsehr**tar**	
menu	a ementa	eemeñtuh	
set menu	a ementa fixa	eemeñtuh **feek**suh	
à la carte	a ementa a	eemeñtuh a	
	la carte	la kart	
menu	la carte	la kart	
message	a mensagem	meñ**sah**-zhayñ	
metre	o metro	**met**roo	
midday	o meio-dia	**mayoo-dee**-uh	
at midday	ao meio-dia	ow **mayoo-dee**-uh	
middle	o meio	**mayoo**	
midnight	a meia-noite	**may**uh-noyt	
at midnight	à meia-noite	a **may**uh-noyt	
mile	a milha	**meel**-yuh	
milk	o leite	layt	
full-cream milk	o leite gordo	layt **gor**-doo	

English	Portuguese	Pronunciation
semi-skimmed milk	o leite meio-gordo	layt **may**oo **gor**doo
skimmed milk	o leite magro com leite	layt **mah**groo koñ layt
with milk	com leite	sayñ layt
without milk	sem leite	okoo**par**-suh duh
million	o milhão	
to mind (take care of)	ocupar-se de	eeñ**por**tuh-suh?
do you mind if...?	importa-se?	nowñ muh ee**por**too
I don't mind	não me importo	
minimum	o mínimo	oo **mee**neemoo
minute	o minuto	oo mee**noo**too
Miss...	Menina...	muh-**nee**nuh...
to miss (plane, train, etc)	perder	pehr-**dehr**
missing (lost)	perdido(a)	pehr-**dee**doo(uh)
mistake	o erro	**err**-oo
to mix	misturar	meestoo**rar**
mobile phone	o telemóvel	tuh-luh-**mo**vel

English	Portuguese	Pronunciation
modern	moderno(a)	moo**dehr**noo(uh)
moment: just a moment	um momento	ooñ moo**meñ**too
Monday	a segunda-feira	suh**goon**-duh **fay**ruh
money	o dinheiro	deen-**yay**-roo
I've no money	não tenho dinheiro	nowñ **ten**-yoo deen-**yay**-roo
month	o mês	maysh
this month	este mês	aysht maysh
last month	o mês passado	maysh puh-**sah**-doo
next month	o mês que vem	maysh kee vayñ
more	mais	mysh
more than 3	mais de três	mysh duh traysh
more bread	mais pão	mysh powñ
more wine	mais vinho	mysh **veen**-yoo
morning	a manhã	mun-**yañ**
in the morning	de manhã	duh mun-**yañ**
this morning	esta manhã	**esh**tuh mun-**yañ**

English - Portuguese

English	Portuguese	Pronunciation
tomorrow	amanhã de	amun-**yañ** duh
morning	manhã	mun-**yañ**
most: most of	a maioria de	my-o-**ree**-uh duh
mother	a mãe	**mah**-ee
motor	o motor	mo**tor**
motorbike	a moto	**mo**too
motorway	a auto-estrada	owtoo-**shtrah**-duh
mouth	a boca	**bo**kuh
to move	mexer;	me**shehr**;
	mover	mo**vehr**
Mr	o Senhor	sun-**yor**
Mrs	a Senhora	sun-**yor**uh
Ms	a Senhora	sun-**yor**uh
much	muito(a)	**mwee**too
too much	demais	duh-**mysh**
mugging	o assalto	uh-**sahl**too
muscle	o músculo	**moosh**-kooloo
museum	o museu	moo-**zay**-oo
music	a música	**moo**zeekuh
must (to have to)	dever	de**vehr**
I must	devo	**deh**-voo
we must	devemos	duh-**veh**-moosh
I mustn't	não devo	nowñ **deh**-voo
we mustn't	não devemos	nowñ duh-**veh**-moosh
my	meu (minha)	**may**oo (**meen**-yuh)

N

English	Portuguese	Pronunciation
name	o nome	nom
narrow	estreito(a)	ee**stray**too(uh)
national	nacional	nasyo**nahl**
nationality	a nacionalidade	nasyo-naleedahd
natural	natural	natoo**rahl**
nature	a natureza	natoo-**reh**-zuh
near	perto	**pehr**too
near the bank	perto do banco	**pehr**too doo **buñ**koo
is it near?	fica perto?	feekuh **pehr**too?
necessary	necessário(a)	nussuh-**sar**-yoo(uh)

English	Portuguese	Pronunciation
to need	preciser de	preseezar duh
I need...	preciso de	pre-**seezoo** duh
we need...	precisamos de	preseezah-moosh duh
I need to go	tenho que ir	**ten**-yoo kuh eer
never	nunca	**noon**kuh
I never drink	nunca bebo	**noon**-kuh **beh**boo **veen**yoo
wine	vinho	
new	novo(a)	**noh**-voo(uh)
news	a notícia	no**teesee**uh
(on television)	o noticiário; o telejornal	notesee-**aryoo**; telezhoor**nahl**
newspaper	o jornal	zhoor**nahl**
New Year	o Ano Novo	**ah**-noo **noh**-voo
New Year's Eve	a véspera de Ano Novo	**vesh**-peruh duh **ah**-noo **noh**-voo
New Zealand	a Nova Zelândia	**noh**-vuh zeh-**luñ**dyuh
next	próximo(a)	**prosse**emoo(uh)
next to	ao lado de	ow **lah**-doo duh
next week	a semana que vem	suh-**mah**-nuh kuh vayñ
the next bus	o próximo autocarro	**prosse**emoo owtoo-**karroo**
the next stop	a próxima paragem	**prosse**emuh parah-**zhayñ**
nice (person)	simpático(a)	seeñ-**pah**-teekoo(uh)
(place)	bonito(a)	boo**neetoo**(uh)
night	a noite	noyt
at night	à noite	a noyt
last night	ontem à noite	**oñ**-tayñ a noyt
per night	por noite	poor noyt
tomorrow night	amanhã à noite	amun-**yañ** a noyt
no	não	nowñ
no entry	entrada proibida	eñ**trah**-duh pro-**eebee**duh
no smoking	proibido fumar	proe-**beedoo** foo**mar**

English – Portuguese

English	Portuguese	Pronunciation
no thanks	não, obrigado(a)	nowñ, oh-bree**gah**-doo(uh)
nobody	ninguém	neeñ**gayñ**
noise	o barulho	ba**rool**-yoo
noisy	barulhento(a)	barool-**yeñ**too(uh)
non-alcoholic	não-alcoólico(a)	nowñ-al**ko**leekoo(uh)
none	nenhum(a)	nayñ-**ooñ** (nayñ-**oomuh**)
there's none left	não sobrou nada	nowñ so**broh** **nah**-duh
non-smoker	o/a não-fumador(a)	nowñ foomuh-**dor**(uh)
non-smoking	não-fumador(a)	nowñ foomuh-**dor**(uh)
north	o norte	nort
Northern Ireland	a Irlanda do Norte	eer**lun**duh doo nort
not	não	nowñ
note (letter)	a nota	**no**tuh
nothing	nada	**nah**-duh
nothing else	mais nada	mysh **nah**-duh
notice	o aviso	uh-**vee**soo
now	agora	uh-**gor**uh
nowhere (be)	em nenhum lugar	ayñ nayñ-**ooñ** loo**gar**
(go)	a lugar nenhum	loogar nayñ-**ooñ**
number	o número	**noo**meroo
O	O	
to obtain	obter	ob**tehr**
occasionally	às vezes	ush **veh**-zush
of	de	duh
a bottle of water	uma garrafa de água	**oo**muh garrah-fuh **ahg**-wuh
a glass of wine	um copo de vinho	ooñ **kop**oo duh **veen**-yoo
made of...	feito de...	**fay**-too duh...

English	Portuguese	Pronunciation
off (radio, engine, etc)	desligado(a)	deesh-lee **gah-doo(uh)**
(milk, food, etc)	estragado(a)	eestruh-**gah-doo(uh)**
this meat is off	esta carne está estragada	**eshtuh** karn shta eestruh-**gah-duh**
office	o escritório	eeshkree-**tor-**yoo
often	muitas vezes	**mweeñ**tush **veh-**zush
how often?	quantas vezes?	**kwuñ**tush **veh-**zush?
OK	está bem	shta bayñ
old	velho(a)	**vel-**yoo(uh)
how old are you?	quantos anos tem?	**kwuñ**toosh **ah-**noosh tayñ?
I'm ... years old	tenho ... anos	**ten-**yoo ... **ah-**noosh
on (light, TV)	aceso(a)	uh-**seh-**zoo(uh)
(engine)	a trabalhar	trabal-**yar**
on	em	ayñ
on the table	na mesa	nuh **may-**zuh
on time	a horas	**oruz**
once	uma vez	**oo**muh vesh
at once	imediatamente	eemeh-dee-ah-tuh-**meñt**
only adj	somente	so**meñt**
	único(a)	**oo**neekoo(uh)
open adj	aberto(a)	uh-**behr-**too
to open	abrir	uh-**breer**
or	ou	oh
tea or coffee?	chá ou café?	shah oh kuh-**fe?**
orange adj	cor-de-laranja	kor duh laruñ**zhuh**
orange (fruit)	a laranja	laruñ**zhuh**
orange juice	o sumo de laranja	**soo**moo duh laruñ**zhuh**
order: out of order	fora de serviço; avariado	**for-**uh duh ser**vee**soo; avaree-**ah-**doo
to order (in restaurant)	pedir	pe**deer**

English – Portuguese

English – Portuguese

to organize	organizar	orguh-neezar
other: the other one	o/a outro(a)	oh-troo(truh)
have you any others?	tem outros(as)?	tayñ oh-troosh(trush)?
our	nosso(a)	nossoo(uh)
out	ora	for-uh
he's gone out	ele saiu	ayl sah-yoo
he's out	não está	nowñ shta
outside: it's outside	está lá fora	shta lah for-uh
over (on top of)	sobre	sobruh
to be overbooked	ter mais reservas que lugares	tehr mysh ruh-zehrvush kuh loogah-rush
to overcharge	cobrar a mais	kobrar a mysh
overdone (food)	cozido demais	koozeedoo duh-mysh
to owe	dever	devehr
you owe me...	deve-me...	dev-muh...
I owe you...	devo-lhe...	deh-voo-lyuh...

package	o embrulho	eeñbrool-yoo
package tour	a viagem organizada	vee-ah-zhayñ organeezah-duh
P		
paid	pago(a)	pah-goo(uh)
pain	a dor	dor
painful	doloroso(a)	dolorozoo(uh)
painkiller	o analgésico	anaízheh-zeekoo
pair	o par	par
paper (newspaper)	o papel	puh-pel
	o jornal	zhoornahl
paracetamol	o paracetamol	paruh-seetuh-mol
parcel	a encomenda	eeñkoomeñduh
pardon	desculpe?	dushkoolp?
I beg your pardon!	desculpe-me!	dushkoolp-muh!
parents	os pais	oosh pysh
to park	estacionar	eesh-tassyoonar
parking ticket	a multa	mooltuh
part	a parte	part

partner (business)	o/a sócio(a)	soh-seeoo(uh)
(friend)	o/a companheiro(a)	koñpun-yay-roo(uh)
party (celebration)	a festa	fesh-tuh
party (political)	o partido	parteedoo
passenger	o/a passageiro(a)	passuh-zhay-roo(uh)
passport	o passaporte	passuh-port
pasta	as massas	ush massush
pastry (dough)	a massa	massuh
(cake)	o bolo	bohloo
patient (adj)	paciente	passee-eñt
to pay	quero pagar	kayro puh-gar
I'd like to pay	onde é que se paga?	oñduh e kuh suh pah-guh?
where do I pay?		
payment	o pagamento	paguh-meñtoo
payphone	o telefone público	tuh-luh-fonee poobleekoo

peanut allergy	a alergia a amendoins	alehr-zhee-uh a ameñdooeeñsh
pear	a péra	pay-ruh
pedestrian crossing	a passadeira para peões	passuh-day-ruh paruh peh-oyñsh
pen	a caneta	kuh-neh-tuh
pencil	o lápis	lah-peesh
pension	a pensão	payñ-sowñ
pensioner	o/a reformado(a)	reformah-doo(uh)
people	as pessoas	ush puh-so-ush
pepper (spice)	a pimenta	peemeñtuh
pepper (vegetable)	o pimento	peemeñtoo
per	por	poor
per hour	por hora	poor oruh
perfect	perfeito(a)	pehr-fay-too(uh)
perhaps	talvez	talvesh
person	a pessoa	puh-so-uh
per person	por pessoa	poor puh-so-uh
petrol	a gasolina	gazooleenuh

English – Portuguese

English - Portuguese

pharmacy	a farmácia	farmass-yuh	(photo)	a foto	foto
phone	o telefone	tuh-luh-fonee	piece	o bocado; o pedaço	bookah-doo; puh-dah-ssoo
mobile telephone	o telemóvel	tuh-luh-movel	pig	o porco	porkoo
to phone	telefonar	tuh-luh-fonar	pill	o comprimido	koñpreemeedoo
phone box	a cabine telefónica	kuh-been-uh tuh-luh-foneekuh	to be on the pill	tomar a pílula	toomar uh peelooluh
photocopy	a fotocópia	fotokoh-pyuh	pilot	o/a piloto(a)	peelohtoo(uh)
photograph	a fotografia	footoograh-fee-uh	pink	cor-de-rosa	kor-duh-roh-zuh
to take a photograph	tirar uma fotografia	teerar oomuh footoogruh-fee-uh	pint	= approx. 0.5 litre	
			a pint of beer	uma caneca de cerveja	oomuh kanehkuh duh servay-zhuh
phrasebook	o guia de conversação	ghee-uh duh koñversuh-sowñ	pizza	a pizza	peezuh
			place	o lugar	loogar
to pick (fruit, flowers)	colher	kool-yer	plan	o plano	plun-oo
(to choose)	escolher	eeshkool-yer	to plan	planear	pluh-nezhar
pickpocket	o/a carteirista	kartay-reesh-tuh	plane	o avião	av-yowñ
picture (painting)	o quadro	kwad:roo	plaster (sticking)	o adesivo	adeh-zeevoo
			plaster (for broken limb)	o gesso	zhessoo
			plastic	o plástico	plash-teekoo

English	Portuguese	Pronunciation
platform (railway)	a linha	leen-yuh
play (at theatre)	a peça	peh-suh
to play (sport)	jogar	zhoogar
(musical instrument)	tocar	tookar
(general play)	brincar	breeñkar
pleasant	agradável	agruh-dah-vel
please	por favor; faz favor	poorfuh-vor; fash fuh-vor
pleased: pleased to meet you	prazer em conhecê-lo(a)	pruh-zehr ayñ koon-ye-say-loo(uh)
plenty: plenty of (much)	muito(a)	mweeñtoo(uh)
(many)	muitos(as)	mweeñtoosh (ush)
p.m. (afternoon/ evening)	de tarde	duh tard
(night)	de noite	duh noyt
police (force)	a polícia	poolee-syuh
police station	a esquadra	eesh-kwah-druh
pool	a piscina	peesh-seenuh
poor	pobre	pobree
pork	a carne de porco	karn duh porkoo
port (wine)	o vinho do porto	veen-yoo doo portoo
(seaport)	o porto	portoo
portion	a porção	poor-sowñ
Portugal	Portugal	poortoo-gahl
Portuguese	português (portuguesa)	poortoo-gaysh (poortoo-gay-zuh)
(language)	o português	poortoo-gaysh
possible	possível	poh-see-vel
post: by post	pelo correio	peh-loo koorrayoo
to post	pôr no correio	pohr noo koorrayoo
post office	os correios	koorrayoosh
potato	a batata	butah-tuh
pound (money)	a libra	leebruh
(weight)	= approx. 0.5 kilo	
power	o poder	poodehr

English – Portuguese

English – Portuguese

to prefer	preferir	preh-fer**eer**
pregnant	grávida	**grah**-veeduh
I'm pregnant	estou grávida	shto **grah**-veeduh
to prepare	preparar	preh-par**ar**
prescription	a receita médica	hu-**say**-tuh **med**eekuh
present (gift)	o presente;	pruh-**zeñt**;
	a oferta;	oofehr**tuh**;
	a prenda	**prayn**-duh
pressure	a pressão	pruh**sowñ**
blood pressure	a tensão arterial	tayñ-**sowñ** arteh-**yahl**
tyre pressure	a pressão dos	pruh**sowñ** doosh
	pneus	**pnay**-oosh
pretty	bonito(a)	boo**nee**too(uh)
price	o preço	**pray**-soo
price list	a lista de preços	**leesh**tuh duh **pray**-soosh
private	privado(a)	preev**ah**-doo(uh)
probably	provavelmente	proovavel**meñt**

problem	o problema	proo**bleh**-muh
no problem	não tem	nowñ tayñ
	problema	proo**bleh**-muh
prohibited	proibido(a)	proee-**bee**doo(uh)
pronounce	pronunciar	pronoonsee**ar**
how is this	como se	**koh**-moo suh
pronounced?	pronuncia isto?	pronoon-**see**-uh **eeshtoo**?
to provide	fornecer	foornes**sehr**
public	público(a)	**poob**leekoo(uh)
public holiday	o feriado	fuh-reeah-doo
to pull	puxar	poo**shar**
purse	o porta-moedas	**portuh**-**mway**-dush
to push	empurrar	eeñpoorr**ar**
to put	pôr	por
to put back	repor	ruh-**por**
pyjamas	o pijama	peezhah-muh
Q		
quality	a qualidade	kwal**eed**ahd

English		Portuguese		
quantity	a quantidade	kwuñteeдаhd	railcard	o passe do comboio	passuh doo koñboyoo
to quarrel	discutir	deesh-kooteer	railway	o caminho de ferro	kuh-meen-yoo duh ferr-oo
quarter	o quarto	kwartoo	railway station	a estação de comboio; o caminho de ferro	shtuh-sowñ duh koñboyoo; kuh-meen-yoo duh ferr-oo
question	a pergunta	pehr-goontuh			
queue	a fila;	feeluh;	rain	a chuva	shoovuh
	a bicha	beeshuh	to rain: it's raining	está a chover	shta a shoovehr
to queue	fazer fila	fazehr feeluh			
quick	rápido(a)	rah-peedoo(uh)	raped: I've been raped	fui violado(a)	fwee veeolah-doo(uh)
quickly	depressa	duh-pressuh			
quiet (place)	sossegado(a)	soo-segah-doo(uh)	rare (unique)	raro(a)	rah-roo(uh)
			rare (steak)	mal passado(a)	mal puh-sah-doo(uh)
a quiet room	um quarto tranquilo	ooñ kwartoo truñkweeloo	rate (price)	a taxa	tashuh
quite: it's quite good	é bastante bom	e bushtuñt boñ	rate of exchange	o câmbio	kuñbyoo
quite expensive	é muito caro	e mweeñto kah-roo	raw	cru(a)	kroo(uh)
R					
radio	o rádio	rah-dyoo			

English – Portuguese

English – Portuguese

razor	a máquina de barbear	**mak**eenuh duh barbee**ar**
razor blades	as lâminas de barbear	**luh**meenush duh barbee**ar**
to read	ler	lehr
ready	pronto(a)	proñ~too(uh)
real	real	reh-**ahl**
to realize	perceber	pehr-suh-**behr**
reason	a razão	ruh-**zowñ**
receipt	o recibo	ruh-**see**boo
reception (desk)	a recepção	ruh-sep-**sowñ**
receptionist	o/a recepcionista	ruh-sepsyor-**neesh**-tuh
to recommend	recomendar	ruhkoomeñ**dar**
red	vermelho(a)	vehr-**mel**-yoo(uh)
to reduce	reduzir	ruh-**doozeer**
reduction	o desconto	deesh**koñ**too
to refer to	referir-se a	uh-fereer-suh a
to refund	o reembolso	ruh-ayñ-**bol**soo
to refuse	recusar	ruh-koo**zar**

to register (at hotel)	preencher o registo	pray-eñ**shehr** oo reh-**zheesh**too
registration form	a folha de registo	**fol**-yuh duh reh-zh**eesh**too
to reimburse	reembolsar	ruh-embol**sar**
relation (family)	o/a parente	pareñt
relationship (personal)	as relações	ruh-luh-**soyñsh**
(family)	o parentesco	pareñ**tesh**koo
to remain	ficar	fee**kar**
to remember	lembrar-se de	laymbrar-suh duh
I don't remember	não me lembro	nowñ muh **laym**broo
to remove	retirar	ruh-teer**ar**
rent (house)	a renda; o aluguer	**rayn**-duh; aloo**gehr**
(car)	o aluguer	aloo**gehr**
to rent (house, car)	alugar	aloo**gar**
repair	a reparação	ruh-paruh-**sowñ**
to repair	reparar; consertar	ruh-parar; koñ**seht**ar

English	Portuguese	Pronunciation
to repeat	repetir	ruh-peteer
to report (crime, person)	comunicar	komooneekar
to request	pedir	pedeer
to require	precisar de	preh-seezar duh
reservation	a reserva	ruh-zehrvuh
to reserve	reservar	ruh-zehrvar
reserved	reservado(a)	ruh-zehrvar-doo
rest (repose)	o descanso	deesh-kuñsoo
rest (remainder)	o resto	resh-too
the rest of the wine	o resto do vinho	resh-too doo veen-yoo
to rest	descansar	deesh-kuñsar
restaurant	o restaurante	rushtoh-ruñt
to retire	reformar-se	ruh-foormar-suh
retired	reformado(a)	ruh-foormah-doo(uh)
I'm retired	estou reformado(a)	shto(uh) ruh-foormah-doo(uh)

English	Portuguese	Pronunciation
to return (to go back)	voltar	voltehr
(to give something back)	devolver	duh-volvehr
return ticket	o bilhete de ida e volta	beel-yet deeduh ee voltuh
rice	o arroz	arrosh
rich (person)	rico(a)	reeko(uh)
right (correct)	certo(a)	sehrt-too(uh)
to be right	ter razão	tehr ruh-zowñ
right: on/to the right	à direita	a dee-ray-tuh
ring (for finger)	o anel	uh-nel
to ring (bell)	tocar	tookar
(phone)	telefonar	tuh-luh-fonar
it's ringing	está a tocar	shta a tookar
road	a estrada	shtrah-duh
road map	o mapa das estradas	mah-puh dush shtrah-dush
road sign	o sinal de trânsito	seenahl duh truñzeetoo

English – Portuguese

English – Portuguese

English	Portuguese	Pronunciation
roadworks	as obras na estrada	ush obrush nuh shtrah-duh
roast	assado(a)	uh-ssahdoo(uh)
roll (bread)	o pãozinho	powñzeen-yoo
romantic	romântico(a)	romuñteekoo(uh)
room (in house, hotel)	o quarto	kwartoo
(space)	o espaço	eesh-pah-ssoo
room number	o número do quarto	noomeroo doo kwartoo
room service	o serviço de quarto	serveesoo duh kwartoo
to run	correr	koorrehr

S

English	Portuguese	Pronunciation
sad	triste	treesht
safe (for valuables)	o cofre	kofree
safe	seguro(a)	segooroo(uh)
is it safe?	é seguro?	e segooroo?
safety belt	o cinto de segurança	seeñtoo duh segooruñsuh

English	Portuguese	Pronunciation
salad	a salada	sah-lah-duh
salary	o salário	salaryoo
sale(s)	o saldo	saldoo
salesman/ woman	o/a vendedor(a)	veñdeh-dor(uh)
salt	o sal	sal
same	mesmo(a)	mesh-moo(uh)
sand	a areia	aray-uh
sandwich	a sandes	suñdush
satellite TV	a televisão via satélite	tuh-luh-vezowñ vee-uh suh-teh-leet
Saturday	o sábado	sah-buh-doo
sauce	o molho	mol-yoo
tomato sauce	o molho de tomate	mol-yoo duh to-maht
sausage	a salsicha	salseeshuh
to save (life)	salvar	salvar
to save (money)	poupar	poh-par
to say	dizer	deezehr
scarf (woollen)	o cachecol	kasheekol

English	Portuguese	Pronunciation	English	Portuguese	Pronunciation
school	a escola	eesh-**koh**-luh	second-class adj	de segunda classe	duh suh**goon**-duh klass
Scotland	a Escócia	eesh-**koss**-yuh	to see	ver	vehr
Scottish	escocês (escocesa)	eesh-ko**saysh** (eesh-ko**say**-zuh)	to sell	vender	vayñ**dehr**
sea	o mar	mar	do you sell...?	vende...?	vayñd...?
seafood	os mariscos	ma**reesh**-koosh	to send	mandar	muñ**dar**
to search for	procurar	prokoo**rar**	serious (illness)	sério(a)	**sehr**-yoo(uh)
seasick	enjoado(a)	ayñ-zhooah-doo(uh)		grave	grahv
I get seasick	fico enjoado	**feeko** ayñ-zhooah-doo(uh)	to serve	servir	sehr-**veer**
			in restaurant)	o serviço	serveesoo
seaside	a praia	**pry**-uh	is service included?	o serviço está incluído?	serveesoo shta eeñkloo-eedoo?
at the seaside	na praia	nuh **pry**-uh	service charge	o serviço	serveesoo
season (of year)	a estação	shtuh-**sowñ**	service station	a estação de serviço	shtuh-**sowñ** duh serveesoo
(holiday)	a temporada	tayñporah-duh	several	vários(as)	**var**/yoosh(ush)
in season	da época	duh **eh**-pookuh	sex (gender)	o sexo	**sek**soo
seat (chair)	a cadeira	kuh-**day**-ruh	(intercourse)	o sexo	**sek**soo
(on bus, train, etc)	o lugar	loo**gar**	shade	a sombra	**soñ**bruh
seatbelt	o cinto de segurança	**seeñ**-too duh segooruñsuh	in the shade	à sombra	a **soñ**bruh
second	segundo(a)	se**goon**doo(uh)	to shake (bottle)	sacudir	sakoo**deer**

English – Portuguese

English – Portuguese

shampoo	o champô	shuĩ**poo**	shower	o duche;	doosh;
to share	dividir	deevee**deer**		o chuveiro	shoova**yroo**
to shave	fazer a barba	fa**zehr** uh **barbuh**	to have a shower	tomar um duche	too**mar** ooñ doosh
she	ela	**ay**luh	(rain)	o chuveiro;	shoova**yroo**;
sheet (for bed)	o lençol	layñ**sol**		o aguaceiro	ugwuh-**sayroo**
shellfish	o marisco	ma**reesh**-koo	fechado(a)	fechado(a)	fuh-**shah**-doo(uh)
shirt	a camisa	kuh-**meezuh**			
shoe	o sapato	suh-**pah**-too	to shut (closed)	fechar	fuh-**shar**
shoe shop	a sapataria	sapuh-tuh-**ree**-uh	sick (ill)	doente	doo-**eñt**
			I feel sick	sinto-me mal-disposto(a)	**seen**-too-muh mal deesh-**posht**oo(uh)
shop	a loja	**lo**zhuh			
shop assistant	o/a vendedor(a)	veñdeh-**dor**(uh)	side	o lado	**lah**-doo
shopping centre	o centro comercial	**señ**troo koměhr-**syahl**	side dish	o acompanhamento	uh-koñpun-yuh-**meñ**too
short	curto(a)	**koort**oo(uh)	sightseeing	o turismo	too**reezh**-moo
shorts	os calções	oosh kaisoynsh	to go sightseeing	fazer turismo	fazehr too**reezh**-moo
to shout	gritar	gree**tar**			
show	o espectáculo	eesh-peh-**takooloo**			
to show	mostrar	moosh-**trar**			

English	Portuguese	Pronunciation		English	Portuguese	Pronunciation
sightseeing tour	a excursão	eesh-koor-**sowñ**		size (clothes)	o tamanho	tuh-**mun**-yoo
sign (road-, notice, etc)	o sinal	seenahl		(shoes)	o número	**noo**meroo
to sign	assinar	asseenar		skin	a pele	payl
signature	a assinatura	asseenuh-**too**ruh		skirt	a saia	**sy**-uh
silver	a prata	**prah**tuh		sky	o céu	**say**-oo
similar: similar to	semelhante	a semel-**yuñt** a		to sleep	dormir	doormeer
				to sleep in	dormir até tarde	doormeer uh-**te** tard
simple	simples	**seeñ**pleesh		slow	lento(a)	lentoo(uh)
since (time)	desde que	dezhd kuh		small	pequeno(a)	puh-**kaynoo**(uh)
(because)	porque	poorkuh		smaller	mais pequeno(a)	mysh puh-**kaynoo**(uh)
since Saturday	desde sábado	dezhd sah-buh-doo		smell	o cheiro	shay-roo
				smoke	o fumo	**foo**moo
to sing	cantar	kuñtar		to smoke	fumar	foomar
single (not married)	solteiro(a)	sol**tay**-roo(uh)		I don't smoke	não fumo	nowñ **foo**moo
single	simples	**seeñ**pleesh		can I smoke?	posso fumar?	**posso** foomar?
sir	senhor	sun-**yor**		smoking: no smoking	proibido fumar	proee-**bee**doo foomar
sister	a irmã	eer**mañ**				
to sit	sentar-se	sayñ-**tar**-suh		smooth	liso(a); macio(a)	**lee**soo(uh); masseeoo(uh)

English – Portuguese

English – Portuguese

snack	o lanche	luñsh
to have a snack	comer qualquer coisa	komehr kwalkehr koy-zuh
snow	a neve	nev
to snow	nevar	neh-var
so	tão	towñ
so much	tanto(a)	tuñtoo(uh)
so then	portanto	poortuñtoo
soap	o sabão	sauh-bowñ
sober	sóbrio(a)	sobreeoo
socket (electrical)	a tomada	toomah-duh
sofa	o sofá	soofah
soft	macio(a)	masseeoo(uh)
soft drink	o refrigerante	ruh-freezheruñt
some	alguns (algumas)	algoonsh (algoo-mush)
someone	alguém	algayñ
something	alguma coisa	algoomuh koy-zuh
sometimes	às vezes	ash veh-zush

son	o filho	feel-yoo
song	a canção	kuñsowñ
soon	em breve	ayñ brev
as soon as possible	o antes possível	poo-see-vel
sore	magoado(a)	magooah-doo(uh)
sore throat: I have a sore throat	dói-me a garganta	doy-muh a garguñtuh
sorry: I'm sorry!	lamento; desculpe!	luh-mayntoo: dushkoolp!
soup	a sopa	sopuh
sour	azedo(a)	uh-zeh-doo(uh)
south	o sul	sool
souvenir	a recordação	ruh-koorduh-sowñ
Spain	a Espanha	eesh-pun-yuh
Spanish	espanhol(a)	eesh-pun-yol (eesh-pun-yol(uh))

English	Portuguese	Pronunciation	English	Portuguese	Pronunciation
(language)	o espanhol	eespun-**yol**	**spicy**	picante	peek**uñt**
sparkling	espumoso(a)	espoomo**zoo**(uh)	**to spill**	entornar	eñtor**nar**
sparkling water	a água com gás	**ahg**-wuh koñ gahs	**spirits**	as bebidas alcoólicas	be**bee**dush al**ko**leekush
sparkling wine	o espumante	eespoo**muñt**	**spoon**	a colher	kool-**yer**
to speak	falar	**fah**-luh	**sport**	o desporto	deesh-**por**too
do you speak English?	fala inglês?	eeñ**glaysh**?	**sports shop**	a loja de artigos desportivos	**lo**zhuh duh ar**tee**goosh deesh-**por**tee-oosh
I don't speak Portuguese	não falo português	nowñ **fah**-loo poortoo-**gaysh**	**spring** (season)	a primavera	preemuh-**veh**ruh
special	especial	eesh-pes**syahl**	(coil)	a mola	**mo**luh
speciality	a especialidade	eesh-pessyalee-**dahd**	**square** (in town)	a praça	**prass**uh
speed	a velocidade	velossee**dahd**	**squash** (drink)	o sumo	**soo**moo
speeding	o excesso de velocidade	eh-**seh**-soo duh velossee**dahd**	(game)	o squash	skwosh
speed limit	o limite de velocidade	lee**meet** duh velossee**dahd**	**stadium**	o estádio	**shtah**dyoo
spell: *how do you spell it?*	como se escreve?	**koh**-moo suh shkrev?	**staff**	o pessoal	puh-**swahl**
to spend (money)	gastar	gash-**tar**	**stain**	a nódoa	**no**doh-uh
			stairs	a escada	eesh**kah**-duh
			stamp (postage)	o selo	**se**loo
			to stand	estar em pé	esh-**tar** ayñ pe

to stand up	levantar-se	leh-vuñ**tar**-suh	eeshtreñluh
star (in sky, in films)	a estrela	eeshtreñluh	
to start	começar	koomessar	
starter (in meal)	a entrada	eñ**trah**-duh	
(in car)	o motor de arranque	mootor duh arruñk	
station	a estação	shtuh-**sowñ**	
statue	a estátua	shta**dee**-uh; veezeetuh	
stay	a estadia; a visita		
to stay	ficar	feekar	
I'm staying at a hotel	fico num hotel	**fee**koo nooñ oh-**tel**	
steak	o bife	beef	
medium steak	o bife ao ponto	beefow **poñ**too	
well-done steak	o bife bem-passado	beef bayñ puh-**sah**-doo	
rare steak	o bife mal-passado	beef mal puh-**sah**-doo	
to steal	roubar	ro-**bar**	

to steam	cozer no vapor	kozehr noo vuh-**por**	
step (stair)	o degrau	deh-**gra**-oo	
stereo	o estéreo	shte-ryo	
sterling (pounds)	esterlino(a)	eesh-tehr-**leeno**(uh)	
still (not moving)	imóvel	eemovel	
(not sparkling)	sem gás	sayñ gahs	
(yet)	ainda	a-**eeñ**duh	
stolen	roubado(a)	roh-**bah**-doo(uh)	
stomach	o estômago	**shtoh**-muh-goo	
stomach upset	o mal-estar de estômago	mal esh-**tar** de **shtoh**-muh-goo	
stone	a pedra	pedruh	
(weight)	= approx. 6.5 kg		
to stop (come to a halt)	parar	parar	
(stop doing something)	deixar de fazer alguma coisa	day-**shar** duh fa**zehr** al**goo**muh **koy**-zuh	

English	Portuguese	Pronunciation
store (shop)	a loja	lozhuh
storey	o andar	uñdar
storm	a tempestade	teñp-shtahd
story	a história	eeshtor-yuh
straightaway	imediatamente	eemuh-dee-ah-tuh-meñt
straight on	sempre em frente	sayñpruh ayñ freñt
strange	estranho(a)	eesh-trun-yoo(uh)
strawberry	o morango	mooruñgoo
street	a rua	roo-uh
street map	o mapa das ruas	mah-puh dush roo-ush
strength	a força	forsuh
strong	forte	fort
strong coffee	o café forte	kuh-fe fort
strong tea	o chá forte	shah fort
student	o/a estudante	shtooduñt
student discount	o desconto para estudantes	deeshkoñtoo paruh shtooduñtush
stung	picado(a)	peekah-doo(uh)
suddenly	de repente	duh ruh-peñt
sugar	o açúcar	uh-sookar
sugar-free	sem açúcar	sayñ uh-sookar
suggest	sugerir	soozhereer
suit (men's and women's)	o fato; o conjunto	fah-too; koñzhoontoo
suitcase	a mala	mah-luh
sum	a soma	somuh
summer	o verão	vuh-rowñ
sun	o sol	sol
to sunbathe	tomar banhos de sol	toomar bun-yoosh duh sol
sunblock	o protector solar	kaymuh-dooruh
sunburn	a queimadura de sol	duh sol
Sunday	o domingo	doomeengoo

English – Portuguese

sunglasses	os óculos de sol	**oh**-kooloosh duh sol	
sunny: *it's sunny*	está sol	shta sol	
sunrise	o nascer do sol	nash-**sehr** doo sol	
sunshade	o guarda-sol; o toldo	**gwar**duh sol; **tol**doo	
sunstroke	a insolação	eeñsoluh-**sowñ**	
suntan	o bronzeado	broñ-zeh-**ah**-doo	
supermarket	o supermercado	sooper-merkah-doo	
supper	a ceia	**say**-uh	
sure	seguro(a)	segoo**roo**(uh)	
I'm sure	estou seguro(a)	shto segoo**roo**(uh)	
surname	o apelido	apee**lee**doo	
my surname is…	o meu apelido é…	mayoo apee**lee**doo e…	
surprise	a surpresa	soor**prez**uh	
to survive	sobreviver	sobruh-vee**vehr**	
to swear (bad language)	blasfemar; praguejar	blashfe**mar**; pruh-ge**zhar**	

(in court)	jurar	zhoo**rar**	
to sweat	suar	soo**ar**	
sweet (not savoury)	doce	dohss	
sweetener	o adoçante	adoh**ssuñt**	
to swell (injury etc)	inchar	eeñ**shar**	
to swim	nadar	nuh-**dar**	
swimming pool	a piscina	peesh-**see**nuh	
swimsuit	o fato de banho	**fah**-too duh **bun**-yoo	
to switch off	apagar; desligar	apuh-**gar**; desh-lee**gar**	
to switch on	acender; ligar	asseñ**dehr**; lee**gar**	
swollen (finger, ankle, etc)	inchado(a)	eeñ**shah**-doo(uh)	

T

table	a mesa	**may**-zuh	
tablet (pill)	o comprimido	koñpreemeedoo	
table tennis	o ping-pong	peeñg-poñg	

English	Portuguese	
table wine	o vinho de mesa	veen-yoo duh may-zuh
take (carry)	levar; transportar	luh-var; trooñspoortar
(to grab, seize)	agarrar	agarrar
(medicine etc)	tomar	toomar
(to take someone to)	levar	luh-var
how long does it take?	quanto tempo demora?	kwuñtoo tayñpoo duh-mor-uh?
take-away (food)	para levar	paruh luh-var
to take off (aircraft)	levantar voo	leh-vuñtar voh-oo
to take out (of bag etc)	tirar	teerar
to talk to	conversar com	koñvehrsar koñ
tall	alto(a)	ahltoo(uh)
tart	a tarte	tart
taste	o sabor	suh-bor
to taste	provar	proovar
can I taste it?	posso provar?	posso proovar?
tax	o imposto	eeñposh-too
taxi	o táxi	taksee
tea	o chá	shah
lemon tea	o chá de limão	shah duh leemowñ
tea with milk	o chá com leite	shah koñ layt
to teach	ensinar	ayñ-seenar
teacher	o/a professor(a)	proofessor(uh)
team	a equipa	e-keepuh
teeth	os dentes	oosh deñtush
telephone	o telefone	tuh-luh-fonee
to telephone	telefonar	tuh-luh-fonar
telephone box	a cabine telefónica	kubeen tuh-luh-fonekuh
telephone call	a chamada	shah-mah-duh
telephone card	o cartão telefónico	kartowñ tuh-luh-foneekuh
telephone directory	a lista telefónica	leeshtuh tuh-luh-foneekuh
telephone number	o número de telefone	noomeroo duh tuh-luh-fonee

English – Portuguese

English – Portuguese

English	Portuguese	Pronunciation
television	a televisão	tuh-luh-veezownÑ
to tell	dizer	deezehr
temperature	a temperatura	teñpruh-tooruh
to have a temperature	ter febre	tehr februh
temporary	temporário(a)	tayñporah-reeoo(uh)
tennis	o ténis	teh-neesh
to test (try out)	testar	tesh-tar
than	que	kuh
better than	melhor do que	mel-yor doo kuh
more than you	mais do que tu	mysh doo kuh too
more than five	mais de cinco	mysh duh seeñkoo
to thank	agradecer	uh-gradessehr
thank you/ thanks	obrigado(a)	oh-breegah-dool-duh)
thank you very much	muito obrigado(a)	mweeñto oh-breegah-doo(-duh)

English	Portuguese	Pronunciation
no thanks	não, obrigado(a)	nowñ, ohbreegah-doo(-duh)
that	aquele (aquela)	uh-kayl (uhkeluh)
the (sing)	o (a)	(uh)
(plural)	os (as)	oosh (ush)
theatre	o teatro	tee-ah-troo
theft	o roubo	roh-boo
their	seu (sua)	sayoo (soo-uh)
them (direct object)	os (as)	oosh (ush)
(indirect object)	lhes	lyesh
(after preposition)	eles (elas)	aylush (elush)
then	então	ayñ-townÑ
there (over there)	ali	alee
there is/ there are	há	a
these	estes (estas)	**ayshtesh** (ayshtush)
these ones	estes (estas)	**ayshtesh** (ayshtush)

English	Portuguese	Pronunciation
they	eles (elas)	aylush (elush)
thick	grosso(a)	grossoo(uh)
thin	magro(a)	magroo(uh)
thing	a coisa	koy-zuh
my things	as minhas coisas	meen-yush koy-zush
to think	pensar	pen-sar
(to be of opinion)	achar	uh-shar
thirsty: I'm thirsty	tenho sede	ten-yoo sed
this	este (esta)	aysht(ayshtuh)
this one	este (esta)	aysht(ayshtuh)
those	aqueles (aquelas)	uh-kaylush (uh-kelush)
those ones	aqueles (aquelas)	uh-kaylush (uh-kelush)
throat	a garganta	garguñtuh
through	através de	atruh-vesh duh
to throw away	deitar fora; descartar	day-tar for-uh; deesh-kartar
thunderstorm	o temporal; a tempestade	tayñpoorahl; tayñp-shtahd
Thursday	a quinta-feira	keeñtuh-fayruh
ticket (bus, train) (for cinema, theatre etc)	o bilhete a entrada	beel-yet eñtrah-duh
a single ticket	um bilhete de ida	ooñ beel-yet deeduh
a return ticket	um bilhete de ida e volta	ooñ beel-yet deeduh ee voltuh
ticket office	a bilheteira	beel-yeh-tayruh
tidy	arrumado(a)	arroomah-doo(uh)
to tidy up	arrumar	arroomar
tie	a gravata	gruh-vahtuh
tight	apertado(a)	apehtah-doo(uh)
tile (floor) (wall)	o ladrilho o azulejo	luh-dreel-yoo azoolayzhoo
till (cash desk)	a caixa	ky-shuh
till (until)	até	uh-te

English – Portuguese

English - Portuguese

English	Portuguese	Pronunciation
till 2 o'clock	até às duas	uh-**te** ash **doo**-ush
time (clock)	o tempo; as horas	**tayñ**poo; ush **oruz**
what time is it?	que horas são?	kee **oruz** sowñ?
this time	esta vez	**esh**tuh vesh
timetable	o horário	oh-**rar**yoo
tip	a gorjeta	goor**zhe**tuh
to tip	dar uma gorjeta	dar **oo**muh goor**zhe**tuh
tired	cansado(a)	kuñ**sah**-doo(uh)
to	a	a
to the airport	ao aeroporto	ow uh-ayroo-**por**too
toast (to eat)	a torrada	toor**rah**-duh
(raising glass)	brindar	breeñ**dar**
tobacco	o tabaco	ta**bah**-koo
tobacconist's	a tabacaria	tabakuh-**ree**-uh
today	hoje	ohzh
together	untos	**zhoon**toosh

English	Portuguese	Pronunciation
toilet	a casa de banho; o lavabo	**kah**-zuh duh **bun**-yoo; luh-**vah**-boo
disabled toilets	a casa de banho para deficientes	**kah**-zuh duh **bun**-yoo **pa**ruh duh-**feess**-**yeñsh**
toilet paper	o papel higiénico	puh-**pel**-ee-zhee-**eh**-nee-koo
toll (motorway)	a portagem	por**tah**-zhayñ
tomato	o tomate	to-**maht**
tomato juice	o sumo de tomate	**soo**moo duh to-**maht**
tomato sauce	o molho de tomate	**mol**-yoo duh to-**maht**
tomorrow	amanhã	amun-**yañ**
tomorrow morning	amanhã de manhã	amun-**yañ** duh mun-**yañ**
tomorrow afternoon	amanhã à tarde	amun-**yañ** a tard

English	Portuguese	Pronunciation
tomorrow evening	amanhã ao fim da tarde/ à noite	amun-**yañ** ow feeñ duh tard/ a noyt
tomorrow night	amanhã à noite	amun-**yañ** a noyt
tonic water	a água tónica	**ahg**-wuh **to**neekuh
tonight	esta noite	**esh**tuh noyt
too (also)	também	tuñ**bayñ**
too big	grande demais	gruñd duh-**mysh**
too small	pequeno(a) demais	puh-**kaynoo**(uh) duh-**mysh**
too noisy	demasiado barulhento(a)	demazyah**doo** barool-**yeñ**too(uh)
tooth	o dente	deñt
top: the top floor	o último andar	**ool**teemoo uñ**dar**
on top of...	em cima de...	ayñ **seem**uh duh...
total (amount)	o total	too**tahl**
to touch	tocar	to**kar**

English	Portuguese	Pronunciation
tour (trip)	a excursão	eeshkoor**sowñ**
(of museum etc)	a visita	ve**zee**tuh
guided tour	a visita guiada	ve**zee**tuh ghee-**ah**-duh
tour guide	o/a guia turístico(a)	toree**shtee**koo (uh)
tour operator	a empresa de viagens	eñ**preh**-zuh duh vee-**ah**-zhayñsh
tourist	o/a turista	tooree**shtuh**
tourist information	a informação turística	eeñfoormuh-**sowñ** tooree**shtee**kuh
tourist office	o posto de turismo	**posh**-too duh tooreezh-moo
town	a cidade	see**dahd**
town centre	o centro da cidade	**señ**troo duh see**dahd**
town hall	a Câmara Municipal	**kum**uh-ruh mooneeseepahl

English - Portuguese

English – Portuguese

English	Portuguese	Pronunciation
town plan	o mapa da cidade	**mah**-puh duh seedahd
toxic	tóxico(a)	**tok**seekoo(uh)
toy	o brinquedo	breeñ**keh**-doo
toy shop	a loja de brinquedos	lozhuh duh breeñ**keh**-doosh
traditional	tradicional	truh-deessyo**nahl**
traffic	o trânsito	**truñ**zeetoo
traffic jam	o engarrafamento	eeñgarrafuh-**meñ**too
traffic lights	o semáforo	semah-fooroo
traffic warden	o/a guarda de trânsito	**gwar**duh duh **truñ**zeetoo
train	o comboio	koñ**boy**oo
by train	de comboio	duh koñ**boy**oo
the next train	o próximo comboio	**pross**eemoo koñ**boy**oo
the first train	o primeiro comboio	pree**may**-roo koñ**boy**oo
the last train	o último comboio	**ool**teemoo koñ**boy**oo
tram	o eléctrico	eletreekoo
to transfer	transferir	truñsfe**reer**
to translate	traduzir	tradoo**zeer**
translation	a tradução	tradoo**sowñ**
to travel	viajar	veeuh-**zhar**
travel agent	o agente de viagens	uh-**zheñt** duh vee-**ah**-zhayñsh
travel insurance	o seguro de viagem	se**goo**roo duh vee-**ah**-zhayñ
traveller's cheque	o cheque de viagem	shek duh vee-**ah**-zhayñ
trip	a viagem	vee-**ah**-zhayñ
trolley (luggage, shopping)	o carrinho	kuh-**reen**-yoo
trouble	os problemas	proo**bleh**-mush
to be in trouble	estar em dificuldades	esh-**tar** ayñ deefeekool**dah**-dush
trousers	as calças	**kahl**ssush

English	Portuguese	Pronunciation
true	verdadeiro(a)	vehr-duh-**day**roo(uh)
to try (attempt)	tentar	tayñ-**tar**
to try on (clothes, shoes)	provar	proo**var**
T-shirt	a T-shirt; a camiseta	t-shirt; kame**zeh**-tuh
Tuesday	a terça-feira	tehr-suh-**fay**ruh
to turn	voltar; girar	vol**tar**; zheer**ar**
to turn around	voltar-se	vol**tar**-suh
to turn off (light)	apagar	apuh-**gar**
(engine)	desligar	desh-leegar
(tap)	fechar	fuh-**shar**
to turn on (light)	acender	asseñ**dehr**
(engine)	ligar	lee**gar**
(tap)	abrir	uh-**breer**
twice	duas vezes	**doo**-ush veh-zush
twin-bedded room	o quarto com duas camas	**kwar**too koñ **doo**-ush **ku**mush

English	Portuguese	Pronunciation
typical	típico	**tee**peekoo
U		
ugly	feio(a)	**fay**-oo(uh)
umbrella	o guarda-chuva; a sombrinha	**gwar**duh **shoo**vuh; soñ**breen**-yuh
(sunshade)	o guarda-sol	**gwar**duh-sol
uncomfortable	incómodo(a)	eeñ**koño**doo(uh)
under	debaixo de	duh-**by**-shoo duh
underground	o metropolitano	metropolee**tuh**-noo
(metro)		
to understand	comprender	koñpreñ-ayñ-**dehr**
I don't understand	não percebo	nowñ pehr-**seh**-boo
do you understand?	percebe?	pehr-**seh**-bee?
underwear	a roupa interior	**roh**-puh eeñtehr-**yor**
to undress	despir-se	dush-**peer**-suh

English – Portuguese

unemployed	desempregado(a) duh-zaympreh-**gah**-doo(uh)	useful	útil **oo**teel
United Kingdom	o Reino Unido **ray**-noo ooneedoo	usual	habitual abeet**wahl**
United States	os Estados Unidos eesh-**tah**doozoo-**nee**doosh	usually	geralmente zhehral**meñt**
to unlock	destrancar deesh-truñ**kar**	**V**	
to unpack (suitcases)	desfazer as malas deesh-fa**zehr** ush **mal**ush	vacancies (in hotel etc)	os quartos kwar**toosh**
unpleasant	desagradável dezagruh-**dah**vel	(jobs)	as vagas **vah**-gush
(person)	antipático(a) uñteepahteekoo (uh)	vacant (hotel room)	o quarto vago **kwar**too **vah**-goo
until	até uh-**te**	vacation	as férias **fehr**-yush
until 2 o'clock	até às duas uh-te ash **doo**ush	on vacation	de férias duh **fehr**-yush
unusual	incomum eeñko**mooñ**	valid	válido(a) **vah**-leedoo(uh)
up: to get up	levantar-se leh-vuñ**tar**-suh	valuable	valioso(a) valee-**oz**oo(uh)
urgent	urgente oor-**zheñt**	valuables	os objetos de valor obzhe**toosh** duh va**lor**
us (after preposition)	nos noosh	value	o valor va**lor**
	nós nosh	VAT	o IVA **ee**vah
to use	utilizar ooteelee**zar**	vegan	vegetalista veh-zhuh-tal**eeshtuh**

English	Portuguese	Pronunciation
I'm vegan	sou vegetalista	soh-veh-zhuh-taleesh**tuh**
vegetables	os legumes; os vegetais	legoomush; veh-zhuh-zhuh-**tysh**
vegetarian	vegetariano(a)	veh-zhuh-tuh-ryah-noo(uh)
I'm vegetarian	sou vegetariano(a)	soh veh-zhuh-tuh-n**yah**-noo(uh)
very	muito	**mwee**too
video camera	a câmara de vídeo	**kum**-ruh duh **vee**-day-oo
view	a vista	**veesh**-tuh
village	a aldeia	al-**day**-uh
vinegar	o vinagre	veen**ah**gruh
visa	o visto	**veesh**too
visit	a visita	veez**ee**tuh
to visit	visitar	veezee**tar**
visitor	a visita	veez**ee**tuh
to vomit	vomitar	voomee**tar**
voucher	o vale; o recibo	val; reh-**see**boo

W

to wait for	esperar por	eesh-peh-**rar** poor
waiter/ waitress	o empregado(a) de mesa	ayñpreh-**gah**-doo(duh) duh **may**-zuh
waiting room	a sala de espera	**sah**-luh duh shpeh-ruh
to wake up	acordar	akoor**dar**
Wales	o País de Gales	pah-**eesh** duh **gal**eesh
to walk	andar	uñ**dar**
walk	o passeio	puh-**say**-oo
wall (inside)	a parede	pa**red**
wall (outside)	o muro	**moo**roo
wallet	a carteira	kar-**tay**-ruh
to want	querer	kay**rehr**
I want...	quero...	**kay**roo...
we want...	queremos...	kay**re**moosh...
warm	quente	keñt
I'm warm	estou com calor	shto koñ ka**lor**

English – Portuguese

English - Portuguese

English	Portuguese	Pronunciation	English	Portuguese	Pronunciation
it's warm (weather)	está calor	shta ka**lor**	week	a semana	suh-**mah**-nuh
to warm up	aquecer	akuh-**sehr**	last week	a semana passada	suh-**mah**-nuh puh-**sah**-duh
to wash	lavar	la**var**	next week	a semana que vem	suh-**mah**- nuh kuh vayñ
watch	o relógio	ruh-**lozh**-yoo	per week	por semana	poor suh-**mah**-nuh
water	a água	**ahg**-wuh	this week	esta semana	**esh**tuh suh-**mah**-nuh
sparkling water	a água com gás	**ahg**-wuh koñ gahs	weekend	o fim-de-semana	feeñ-duh-suh-**mah**-nuh
still water	a água sem gás	**ahg**-wuh sayñ gahs	next weekend	o próximo fim-de-semana	**prosse**emoo feeñ-duh-suh-**mah**-nuh
watermelon	a melancia	meluñ**see**-uh	this weekend	este fim-de-semana	aysht feeñ-duh-suh-**mah**-nuh
way in (entrance)	a entrada	eñ**trah**-duh	weekly	por semana	poor suh-**mah**-nuh
way out (exit)	a saída	sah-**ee**duh	weekly ticket	o bilhete semanal	beel-**yet** suh-muh-**nahl**
we	nós	nosh	to weigh	pesar	peh-**zar**
weak (tea, etc)	fraco(a)	**frah**koo(uh)			
to wear	vestir	veshteer			
weather	o tempo	**tayñ**-poo			
weather forecast	a previsão do tempo	preh-veezo**wñ** doo **tayñ**-poo			
wedding	o casamento	kuzuh-**mayñ**-too			
Wednesday	a quarta-feira	kwartuh-**fayr**uh			

English	Portuguese	
weight	o peso	peh-zoo
welcome	bem-vindo(a)	bayñ-veeñ-doo(uh)
well	bem	bayñ
he's not well	ele não se sente	ayl nowñ suh señt
Welsh	galês (galesa)	galaysh (galay-zuh)
(language)	o galês	galaysh
west	o oeste	oaysht
wet	molhado(a)	mool-yah-doo(uh)
(weather)	chuvoso(a)	shoovozoo(uh)
what	que	kuh
what is it?	o que é?	kuh e?
when?	quando?	kwuñdoo?
where?	onde?	oñduh?
which: which is it?	qual é?	kwal e?
while	enquanto	ayñ-kwuñtoo

English	Portuguese	
in a while	dentro de pouco	deñtroo duh pohkoo
white	branco(a)	bruñkoo(uh)
who: who is it?	quem é?	kayñ e?
whole	inteiro(a)	eeñ-tay-roo(uh)
wholemeal bread	o pão integral	powñ eeñteh-grahl
whose: whose is it?	de quem é?	duh kayñ e?
why?	porquê?	poor-kuh?
wide	largo(a)	largoo(uh)
width	a largura	largooruh
wife	a mulher; a esposa	mool-yehr; shpozuh
to win	ganhar	gun-yar
wind	o vento	veñtoo
window	a janela	zhuh-neluh
(shop)	a montra	moñtruh
wine	o vinho	veen-yoo
red wine	o vinho tinto	veen-yoo teeñtoo

English – Portuguese

white wine	o vinho branco	**veen**-yoo **bruñ**koo
rosé wine	o vinho rosé	**veen**-yoo roh-**ze**
dry wine	o vinho seco	**veen**-yoo **seh**-koo
sparkling wine	o vinho espumante	**veen**-yoo eesh-poo**muñt**
winter	o inverno	eeñ**vehr**-noo
with	com	koñ
with ice	com gelo	koñ **zhe**loo
without	sem	sayñ
without sugar	sem açúcar	sayñ uh-**soo**kar
woman	a mulher	mool-**yehr**
word	a palavra	palah-vruh
to work (person)	trabalhar	trabal-**yar**
(machine)	funcionar	foonss-yo**nar**
it doesn't work	não está a funcionar; não funciona	nowñ shta uh foonss-yo**nar**; nowñ foonss-**yo**nuh
world	o mundo	**moon**doo

worried	preocupado(a)	preh-okoopah-doo(uh)
worse	pior	pee-**or**
to wrap (parcel)	embrulhar	ayñbrool-**yar**
to write	escrever	eesh-kreh-**vehr**
please write it down	escreve-o por favor	eesh-**kreh**-veh-oo poor fuh-**vor**
wrong	errado(a)	e**rrah**-doo(uh)
X		
x-ray	a radiografia	rah-dyoo-grafee-uh
to x-ray	radiografar	rah-dyoo-gra**far**
Y		
year	o ano	**ah**-noo
last year	o ano passado	**ah**-noo puh-**sah**-doo
next year	o ano que vem	**ah**-noo kuh vayñ
this year	este ano	aysht **ah**-noo

yearly: *twice* / yearly	duas vezes por ano	**doo**-ush veh-zush poor **ah**-noo
yellow / Yellow Pages	amarelo(a) / as Páginas Amarelas	amareh-loo(uh) ush **pah**-zheenush amareh-lush
yes	sim	seeñ
yesterday	ontem	**oñ**-tayñ
yet: *not yet*	ainda não	a-**eeñ**duh nowñ
you	você/tu/ vocês/vós	voh-**say**/too/ voh-**saysh**/vosh
young (person)	novo(a) / o/a jovem	**noh**-voo(uh) **zho**vayñ
your	seu (sua)/ teu (tua)/ seu (sua)/ vosso(a)	sayoo (**soo**-uh)/ tayoo (**too**-uh)/ sayoo (**soo**-uh)/ **voss**oo(uh)
youth hostel	o albergue da juventude	al**behr**-guh duh zhuvayñ**tood**

Z

zone	a zona	**zo**nuh
zoo	o jardim zoológico	zhuhr**deeñ** zoh-olo**zhee**koo

English – Portuguese

Portuguese - English

Portuguese	English
a	to; the *(feminine)*
abaixo	down; below
aberto	open
aberto todo o ano	open all year round
abrir	to open; to unlock *(door)*
acabar	to end; to finish
aceitar	to accept
achar	to think; to find
acha bem?	do you think it's all right?
acima	above
acordo *m*	agreement
Açores *mpl*	the Azores archipelago
actual	present(-day)
açúcar *m*	sugar
adega *f*	wine cellar
adeus	goodbye
adiantado(a)	fast *(watch)*; early *(train, etc)*
advogado(a) *m/f*	lawyer
aéreo(a):	airline
a linha aérea	airline
via aérea	air mail
agora	now
agradável	pleasant
agradecer	to thank
água *f*	water
aguardente *f*	spirit brandy
ajudar	to help
albergue *m*	hostel
albergue da juventude	youth hostel
alegre	jolly
alface *f*	lettuce
alfândega *f*	customs
algum(a)	some; any
alguns (algumas)	a few; some
mais alguma coisa?	anything else?
alho *m*	garlic
alhos-porros *mpl*	leeks
ali	there
almoço *m*	lunch
pequeno-almoço m	breakfast
alto!	stop!
alto(a)	high; tall; loud
a estação alta	high season
altura *f*	height
alugar	to hire; to rent
aluga-se	to rent
alugam-se quartos	rooms to let
aluguer *m*	rental
amanhã	tomorrow
amarelo(a)	yellow
amargo(a)	bitter
amêijoa *f*	clam; cockle
amigo(a) *m/f*	friend

Portuguese	English
analgésico *m*	painkiller
ananás *m*	pineapple
andar *m*	to walk
o primeiro andar	floor; storey; first floor
aniversário *m*	anniversary; birthday
ano *m*	year
Ano Novo	New Year
antes (de)	before
apagar	to switch/turn off (*light, etc*)
apelido *m*	surname
apelido de solteira	maiden name
apenas	only
apetite *m*	appetite
bom apetite!	enjoy your meal!
apólice de seguro *f*	insurance certificate
aquecedor *m*	heater; electric fire
aquecimento *m*	heating
aqui	here
ar *m*	air; choke (*car*)
ar condicionado	air conditioning
arder	to burn
areia *f*	sand
arroz *m*	rice
árvore *f*	tree
ascensor *m*	lift
assado(a)	roast; baked
assinar	to sign
assinatura *f*	signature
até	until; as far as
atrás	behind
atrasado(a)	late (*for appointment*)
atrasar	to delay
atravessar	to cross
atum *m*	tuna (fish)
autocarro *m*	bus; coach
a paragem de autocarro	bus stop
auto-estrada *f*	motorway
autorização *f*	licence; permit
avariado(a)	out of order (*machine*); broken down (*car*)
avião *m*	plane
aviso *m*	warning
avô *m*	grandfather
avó *f*	grandmother
azedo(a)	sour
azeite *m*	olive oil
azeitona *f*	olive
azul	blue
azulejo *m*	ornamental tile

B

bacalhau *m*	dried salt cod

Portuguese – English

Portuguese – English

bagagem f	luggage; baggage	beber	to drink	boa
baixo: em baixo	below	bebida f	drink	boca f
balcão m	shop counter; circle in theatre	belo(a)	beautiful	bola f
		bem	well	bolacha f
banco m	bank; seat (in car, etc)	está bem	OK	bolo m
		bem passado	well done (steak)	bolsa f
banho m	bath	bem-vindo(a)	welcome	
a casa de banho	bathroom	berço m	crib; cradle; cot	bom (boa)
tomar banho	to have a bath	bica f	espresso coffee	bom dia
barato(a)	cheap	bicha f	queue	boa tarde
barco m	boat; ship	fazer bicha	to queue	boa noite
barriga f	belly	bife m	steak	
barulho m	noise	bife com batatas fritas	steak and chips	bombeiros mpl
bastante	enough			bonito(a)
batata f	potato	bilhete m	ticket; fare	borrego m
bater	to beat; to knock	bilhete de entrada	admission	braço m
bata à porta	please knock	bilhete de identidade	ticket	branco(a)
batido de leite m	milk shake		identity card	breve
baunilha f	vanilla	bilheteira f	ticket office	em breve
bebé m	baby			

boa	see **bom**
boca f	mouth
bola f	ball
bolacha f	biscuit
bolo m	cake
bolsa f	stock exchange; handbag
bom (boa)	good; fine
bom dia	(weather); kind good morning
boa tarde	good afternoon
boa noite	good evening; good night
bombeiros mpl	fire brigade
bonito(a)	pretty
borrego m	lamb
braço m	arm
branco(a)	white
breve	brief
em breve	soon

Portuguese – English

britânico(a) — British
broa f — corn (maize) bread
bronzeador m — suntan oil
buscar — to look for

C

cabeça f — head
cabeleireiro(a) m/f — hairdresser
cabelo m — hair
cabine f — cabin; booth
cabine telefónica — phone box
cada — each; every
cadeira f — chair
cadeira de bebé — high chair; push chair
cadeira de rodas — wheelchair
café m — (black) coffee; café

cair — to fall; to fall over
caixa f — cash desk
caixa — cash machine
caixa automática
caixa do correio — letterbox
calar — to stop talking; to keep silent
calçado m — footwear
calças fpl — trousers
calções mpl — shorts
calções de banho — swimming trunks
calcular — to estimate; to calculate
calor m — heat
cama f — bed
cama de casal — double bed
cama de bebé — cot
cama de solteiro — single bed
a roupa de cama — bedding

câmara municipal f — town hall
cambiar — to exchange; to change money
câmbio m — exchange rate
casa de câmbios f — exchange bureau
camião m — lorry
camioneta f — coach
camisa f — shirt
camisa de noite — nightdress
campismo m — camping
campo m — field; countryside
cancelar — to cancel
caneta f — pen
cansaço m — fatigue
cansado(a) — tired
cantar — to sing
cão m — dog
capacete m — crash helmet

Portuguese – English

capela f	chapel	carteirista m	pickpocket	cêntimo m	cent
cara f	face	casa f	home; house	centro m	centre
caranguejo m	crab	casa de banho	toilet; bathroom	centro da cidade	city centre
carioca	weak coffee	casaco m	jacket; coat	centro comercial	shopping centre
carioca de limão	lemon infusion	casado(a)	married	centro de saúde	health centre
carne f	meat	casal m	couple		
carnes frias	cold meats	casamento m	wedding	cereja f	cherry
caro(a)	expensive	caso m	case	certeza f	certainty
caro(a) amigo(a)	dear friend	em caso de...	in case of...	ter a certeza	to be sure
carro m	car	castanho(a)	brown	certo(a)	right (correct, accurate);
carta f	letter	castelo m	castle		certain
cartão m	card; business card	catedral f	cathedral	cerveja f	beer; lager
cartão bancário	cheque card	causa f	cause	céu m	sky
		por causa de	because of	chá m	tea
cartão de crédito	credit card	cavalheiro m	gentleman	chamada f	telephone call
		cave f	cellar	chamada gratuita	free call
cartão de embarque	boarding card	cebola f	onion		
cartão garantia	cheque card	cedo	early		
carteira f	wallet	cego(a)	blind		
		cem	one hundred		
		cenoura f	carrot		

Portuguese	English
chamada internacional	international call
chamada pagável no destino	reverse charge call
chamar	to call
charcutaria f	delicatessen
chave f	key
fechar à chave	to lock up
chefe m	boss
chegadas fpl	arrivals
chegar	to arrive
cheio(a)	full
cheirar	to smell
cheiro m	smell
cheque m	cheque
cheque de viagem	traveller's cheque
levantar um cheque	to cash a cheque
churrascaria f	barbecue restaurant
churrasco m	barbecue
chuva f	rain
cidade f	town; city
cigarro m	cigarette
cima: em cima de	on (top of)
cinto m	belt
cinto de salvação	lifebelt
cinto de segurança	seat belt
cinzento(a)	grey
claro(a)	light (colour); bright
cobrar	to cash; charge
cobrir	to cover
código m	code; dialling code
código postal	postcode
cofre m	safe
coisa f	thing
colégio m	(secondary) school
colete de salvação m	life jacket
com	with
comando m	TV remote control
comboio m	train
combustível m	fuel
começar	to begin; to start
comer	to eat
comida f	food
como	as; how
como disse?	I beg your pardon?
como está?	how are you?
companheiro(a) m/f	live-in partner
companhia (Cia.) f	company

Portuguese – English

Portuguese – English

completar	to complete	
completo	no vacancies *(sign in hotel, etc)*	
compra *f*	purchase	
ir às compras	to go shopping	
comprar	to buy	
compreender	to understand	
comprimido *m*	pill; tablet	
computador *m*	computer	
concordar	to agree	
condução *f*	driving	
a carta de condução	driving licence	
condutor *m*	driver; chauffeur	
conduzir	to drive	
conferir	to check	
congelado(a)	frozen *(food)*	
congelar	to freeze	
não congelar	do not freeze	
conhaque *m*	cognac	

conhecer	to know *(person, place)*	
consertos *mpl*	repairs	
conservar	to keep; to preserve	
conservar no frio	store in a cold place	
constipação *f*	cold *(illness)*	
consulta *f*	consultation; appointment	
consultório *m*	surgery	
consumir antes de...	best before... *(label on food)*	
conta *f*	account; bill	
conter	to contain	
não contem...	does not contain...	
contra	against	
contrato *m*	contract	
convidar	to invite; to ask *(invite)*	

copo *m*	glass *(container)*	
cor *f*	colour	
coração *m*	heart	
cordeiro *m*	lamb	
corpo *m*	body	
correio *m*	post office	
pelo correio	by post	
correr	to flow; to run *(person)*	
cortar	to cut; to cut off	
cortar e fazer brushing	to cut and blow-dry	
corte *m*	cut	
costeleta *f*	chop *(meat)*; cutlet	
couve *f*	cabbage	
couvert *m*	cover charge	
cozinha *f*	kitchen	
cozinhar	to cook	
creme *m*	custard	

creme de barbear	shaving cream
creme para bronzear	suntan cream
criança *f*	child
cru(a)	raw
cruzamento *m*	junction (crossroads)
cuidado *m*	care (caution)
cumprimento *m*	greeting
cumprimentos	regards
curso *m*	course
curto(a)	short
curva *f*	bend; turning; curve
curva perigosa	dangerous bend
custar	to cost
custo *m*	charge; cost

D

dano *m*	damage

dar	to give
dar prioridade	to give way
data *f*	date
data de nascimento	date of birth
de	of; from
debaixo de	under
deficiente	disabled
degrau *m*	step (stair)
deitar-se	to lie down
deixar	to let (allow); to leave behind
delito *m*	crime
demais	too much; too many
demorado(a)	late
demorar	to delay
dente(s) *m*	tooth/teeth
dentro	inside
depois	after(wards)

depósito *m*	deposit (in bank)
depósito de bagagens	left-luggage
depósito da gasolina	petrol tank
depressa	quickly
desaparecido(a)	missing
descansar	to rest
descer	to go down
desculpe	excuse me; sorry
desejar	to desire; to wish
desligado(a)	off (engine, gas)
desligar	to hang up (phone); to switch off (engine, radio)
desmaiar	to faint
despesa *f*	expense
desporto *m*	sport

Portuguese – English

Portuguese – English

devagar	slowly; slow down (sign)	
dever: eu devo	I must	
devolver	to give back; to return	
dia m	day	
dias da semana	weekdays	
dia útil	working day	
dia de anos	birthday	
diário	daily	
diarreia f	diarrhoea	
dieta f	diet; special diet	
diferença f	difference	
difícil	difficult	
digestão f	digestion	
diminuir	to reduce	
dinheiro m	money; cash	
direcção f	direction; address; steering	

direita f	right(-hand side)
à direita	on the right
para a direita	to the right
direito(a)	straight; right(-hand)
Dto.	on right-hand side (address)
direitos mpl	duty (tax); rights
disponível	available
dívida f	debt
dizer	to say
dobro m	double
doce adj	sweet (taste)
doente	ill; sick
doer	to ache; to hurt
domicílio m	residence
domingo m	Sunday
dono(a) m/f	owner
dona de casa	housewife
dor f	ache; pain

dormir	to sleep
Dto.	see **direito(a)**
duche m	shower
duplo(a)	double
durante	during
durar	to last
duro(a)	hard; stiff; tough (meat)

E

e	and
é	he/she/it is; you are
ela	she; her; it (feminine)
elas	they (feminine)
ele	he; him; it (masculine)
eléctrico m	tram
electro-domésticos mpl	electrical appliances

Portuguese	English
em	at; in (with towns, countries); into
embaixada f	embassy
ementa f	menu
ementa fixa	set menu
empregado(a) m/f	waiter (waitress); maid attendant (at petrol station); assistant (in shop); office worker
emprego m	job; employment
empurrar	to push
empurre (sign)	push
encher	to fill up; to pump; to pump up (tyre)
enchidos mpl	processed meats; sausages
encontrar	to meet; to find
encontro m	date; meeting
endereço m	address
ensopado m	stew served on slice of bread
enorme	big; huge
entender	to understand
entrada f	entrance; starter (in meal)
entrada livre	admission free
entrar	to go in; to come in; to get into (car, etc)
entre	among; between
enviar	to send
enxaqueca f	migraine
erro m	mistake
ervilhas fpl	peas
escada f	ladder; stairs
escada rolante	escalator
escocês (escocesa)	Scottish
Escócia f	Scotland
escola f	school
escrever	to write
escritório m	office
escuro(a)	dark (colour)
escutar	to listen to
esgotado(a)	sold out (tickets); exhausted
espaço m	space
Espanha f	Spain
espanhol m	Spanish (language)
espanhol(a)	Spanish
esparguete m	spaghetti
esperar	to expect; to hope
esperar por	to wait for
esposa f	wife
espumante m	sparkling wine
esquerda f	left (-hand side)
à esquerda	on the left

Portuguese – English

Portuguese - English

Portuguese	English
Esq.	on left(-hand) side (address)
está	he/she/it is; you are
estação f	station; season
estação alta	high season
estação baixa	low season
estação do ano	season
estação de autocarros	bus station
estação de serviço	service station
estação do comboio	railway station
estacionamento m	parking
estacionar	to park (car)
Estados Unidos (EUA) mpl	United States
estar	to be
este/esta m/f	this
estes/estas m/f	these
estômago m	stomach
estrada f	road
estrada nacional (EN)	major road; national highway
estrada secundária	minor road
estrangeiro(a) m/f	foreigner
estranho(a)	strange
estudante m/f	student
etiqueta f	ticket; label; etiquette
eu	I
excesso de bagagem m	excess luggage; excess baggage
excursão f	excursion; tour
excursão guiada	guided tour
explicar	to explain

F

Portuguese	English
fácil	easy
factura f	invoice
fado m	traditional Portuguese song
falar	to speak
falta f	lack
falta de corrente	power cut
farmácia f	chemist's
farmácia permanente	duty chemist
farmácias de serviço	emergency chemists'
fato m	suit (man's)
fato de banho	swimsuit
fato de treino	tracksuit
favas fpl	broad beans
fazer	to do; to make
febre f	fever
febre dos fenos	hay fever

Portuguese	English
ter febre	to have a temperature
fechado	closed
fechado Domingos e Feriados	closed Sundays and Bank holidays
fechar	to shut; to close
feijão m	beans
feio(a)	awful; ugly
feira f	fair (commercial); market
feliz	happy
feriado m	public holiday
feriado nacional	bank holiday
férias fpl	holidays
festa f	party (celebration)
Fevereiro m	February
ficar	to stay; to be; to remain
ficar bem	to suit
fila f	row (line); queue
filha f	daughter
filho m	son
fim m	end
fim-de-semana	weekend
flor f	flower
fogo m	fire
fome f	hunger
fora	out; outside
força f	power (strength); force
forte	strong
fotografia f	photograph; print
fraco(a)	weak
frango m	chicken (young and tender)
freguês (freguesa) m/f	customer
frente f	front
em frente de	in front of; opposite
fresco(a)	fresh; cool; crisp
sirva fresco	serve cool
frigorífico m	fridge
frio(a)	cold
fritar	to fry
frito(a)	fried
fruta f	fruit
fumadores mpl	smokers
para não fumadores	non-smoking (compartment, etc)
fumar	to smoke
não fumar	no smoking
fumo m	smoke
funcionar	to work (machine)
não funciona	out of order (sign)
fundo(a)	deep

Portuguese – English

Portuguese – English

G

gabinete de provas *m*	changing room
galão *m*	large white coffee; gallon
galeria *f*	gallery
Gales: o País de Gales	Wales
galês (galesa)	Welsh
ganhar	to earn; to win
garagem *f*	garage
garantia *f*	guarantee
garoto *m*	boy; small white coffee
garrafa *f*	bottle
gás *m*	gas
a botija de gás	gas cylinder
gasóleo *m*	diesel
gasolina *f*	petrol
gasosa *f*	fizzy sweetened water
gastar	to spend
gelado *m*	ice cream; ice lolly
gelo *m*	ice
gente *f*	people
toda a gente	everybody
geral *adj*	general
em geral	generally
geralmente	usually
gerente *m/f*	manager
golfe *m*	golf
o taco de golfe	golf club (stick)
gordo(a)	fat
gorjeta *f*	tip (to waiter, etc)
gostar de	to like
gosto *m*	taste
governo *m*	government
Grã-Bretanha *f*	Britain
grande	big; large; great
grávida	pregnant
gripe *f*	flu
grupo *m*	group; party (group)
grupo sanguíneo	blood group
guarda *m/f*	police officer
guarda-chuva *m*	umbrella
guardar	to keep; to watch over
guia *m/f*	guide
guisado *m*	stew

H

há	there is; there are
habitação *f*	residence; home
hoje	today
homem *m*	man
o wc dos Homens	gents' toilet
hora *f*	hour; time (by the clock)
hora de ponta	rush hour
horário *m*	timetable
hortelã *f*	mint (herb)

hortelã-pimenta f — peppermint

I

ida f — visit; trip; single trip
ida e volta — return trip
idade f — age
identificação f — identification
idosos mpl — the elderly; old people
igreja f — church
igual — equal; the same as
ilha f — island
impedido(a) — engaged (phone)
imperial m — draught beer
imposto m — tax; duty
impostos — duty; tax
impresso m — form (to fill in)
imprevisto(a) — unexpected

incêndio m — fire
incluído(a) — included
incomodar — to disturb
não incomodar — do not disturb
indicativo m — dialling code
infecção f — infection
inflamação f — inflammation
informação f — information
infracção f — offence
Inglaterra f — England
inglês m — English (language)
inglês (inglesa) — English
inscrever — to register
insolação f — heatstroke; sunstroke
inteiro(a) — whole
interessante — interesting
intestinos mpl — bowels
intoxicação f — food poisoning

introduzir — to introduce; to insert
inverno m — winter
ir — to go
Irlanda f — Ireland
a Irlanda do Norte — Northern Ireland
irlandês (irlandesa) — Irish
irmã f — sister
irmão m — brother
IVA m — VAT

J

já — already; now
jamais — never
Janeiro m — January
janela f — window
jantar m — dinner; evening meal
jardim m — garden

Portuguese – English

Portuguese – English

jogar	to play (sport)	lampreia f	lamprey	lembranças fpl	souvenirs
jogo m	match; game; play	laranja f	orange	lençol m	sheet
		o doce de laranja	marmalade	lente f	lens
jornal m	newspaper			lentes de contacto	contact lenses
jovem	young	largo(a)	broad; loose (clothes); wide	lento(a)	slow
Julho m	July				
Junho m	June	largura f	width	ler	to read
juntar	to join	lavabo m	lavatory; toilet	levantar	to draw (money); to lift
junto	near	lavandaria f	laundry		
		lavar	to wash (clothes)	levantar-se	to stand up; get up (from bed)
K		legumes mpl	vegetables		
kg.	see quilo(grama)	lei f	law	levar	to take; to carry
		leitão m	sucking pig	leve	light (not heavy)
L		leite m	milk	libra f	pound
lã f	wool	com leite	white (coffee)	libras esterlinas	pounds sterling
lado m	side	leite desnatado	skimmed milk	licença f	permit
ao lado de	next to	leite evaporado	evaporated milk	ligação f	connection (trains, etc)
ladrão (ladra) m/f	thief	leite gordo	full-cream milk	ligado(a)	on (engine, gas, etc)
lagosta f	lobster	leite magro	skimmed milk		
lagostim m	king prawn	leite meio-gordo	semi-skimmed milk	limão m	lemon

Portuguese – English

limpar — to wipe; to clean
linha f — line; thread; platform (railway)
liquidação f — (clearance) sale
Lisboa (Lx) — Lisbon
lista f — list
lista de preços — price list
lista telefónica — telephone directory
litro m — litre
livraria f — bookshop
livre — free; vacant; for hire
livro m — book
lixo m — rubbish
loja f — shop
lombo m — loin (cut of meat)
longe — far
é longe? — is it far?
longo(a) — long

lotaria f — lottery
louro(a) — fair (hair)
lua-de-mel f — honeymoon
lugar m — seat (theatre); place
lulas f pl — squid
luz f — light
Lx — see Lisboa

M

M. — underground (metro)
má — see mau
maçã f — apple
madeira f — wood
mãe f — mother
magro(a) — thin
Maio m — May
maior — larger
a maior parte de — the majority of

mais — more
o/a mais — the most
mal m — wrong; evil
mala f — suitcase; bag; trunk
mal-estar m — discomfort
mandar — to send; to order
manhã f — morning
manteiga f — butter
manter — to keep; to maintain
mapa m — map
mapa das estradas — road map
mapa das ruas — street plan
máquina f — machine
máquina fotográfica — camera
mar m — sea
maracujá m — passion fruit
Março m — March

Portuguese – English

Portuguese	English
maré f	tide
maré alta f	high tide
maré baixa f	low tide
marido m	husband
marisco m	seafood; shellfish
mas	but
massa f	dough
massas	pasta
matrícula f	number plate
mau (má)	bad; evil
me	me
média f	average
medicamento m	medicine
médico(a) m/f	doctor
médio(a)	medium
medusa f	jellyfish
meia f	stocking; half
meio m	middle
no meio de	in the middle of
meio(a)	half
meio-dia m	midday; noon
melhor	better
o/a melhor	the best
menina f	Miss; girl
menino m	boy
menor	smaller; minor (under age)
menos	least; less
mensagem f	message
mercado m	market
mercearia f	grocer's
mês m	month
mesa f	table
metade f	half
pela metade do preço	half-price
metro m	metre; underground (rail)
metropolitano m	tube (underground)
meu (minha)	my; mine
mexer	to move
não mexer	do not touch
mexilhão m	mussel
mil	thousand
mim	me
minha	see **meu**
mínimo(a)	minimum
moeda f	coin; currency
montanha f	mountain
morada f	address
morango m	strawberry
morar	to live; to reside
morder	to bite
fui mordido(a)	I was bitten
por um cão	by a dog
morrer	to die
mostrar	to show
motocicleta f	motorbike
motor m	engine; motor
motor de arranque	starter motor

motorista *m/f*	driver
mudar	to change
mudar-se	to move house
muito	very; much; quite (*rather*)
muitos(as)	a lot (of); many; plenty (of)
mulher *f*	female; woman; wife
multa *f*	fine
mundo *m*	world

N

nada	nothing
nada a declarar	nothing to declare
nadar	to swim
namorado(a) *m* *f*	boyfriend/girlfriend
não	no; not
nascer	to be born

nascimento *m*	birth
nata *f*	cream
Natal *m*	Christmas
natureza *f*	nature
neblina *f*	mist
negativo(a)	negative
negócios *mpl*	business
nenhum(a)	none
neve *f*	snow
nevoeiro *m*	fog
ninguém	nobody
No.	see **número**
nocivo(a)	harmful
nódoa *f*	stain
noite *f*	evening; night
à noite	in the evening/ at night
boa noite	good evening/ night

noivo(a) *adj*	engaged (to be married)
m/f	bride/groom; fiancé(e)
nome *m*	name
nome próprio	first name
normalmente	usually
nós	we; us
nosso(a)	our
notar	to notice
notícia *f*	piece of news
Nova Zelândia *f*	New Zealand
Novembro *m*	November
novo(a)	new; young; recent
nublado(a)	dull (*weather*); cloudy
número (No.) *m*	number; size (*of clothes, shoes*)
nunca	never

Portuguese – English

Portuguese - English

O

o — the *(masculine)*
objeto *m* — object
objetos perdidos — lost property
obras *fpl* — roadworks; repairs
obrigado(a) — thank you
ocidental — western
oculista *m/f* — optician
óculos *mpl* — glasses
óculos de sol — sunglasses
ocupado(a) — engaged *(phone, toilet)*
oferecer — to offer; to give something
oferta *f* — offer; gift
olá — hello
óleo *m* — oil
óleo dos travões — brake fluid
olhar para/por — to look at/after

olho *m* — eye
onde — where
ontem — yesterday
ordem *f* — order
ou — or
ouro *m* — gold
de ouro — gold *(made of gold)*
outono *m* — autumn
outro(a) — other
outra vez — again
Outubro *m* — October
ouvir — to hear; to listen (to)
ovo *m* — egg

P

padaria *f* — baker's
pagamento *m* — payment
pagamento a pronto — cash payment
pagar — to pay
página *f* — page
páginas amarelas — Yellow Pages
pago(a) — paid
pai *m* — father
pais *m* — parents
país *m* — country
palácio *m* — palace
pane *f* — breakdown
pão *m* — bread; loaf
pão integral — wholemeal bread
pão torrado — toasted bread
pão de trigo — wheat bread
papel *m* — paper
papel higiénico — toilet paper
papelaria *f* — stationer's
par *m* — pair; couple
para — for; towards; to
paragem *f* — stop *(for bus, etc)*

Portuguese	English
parar	to stop
parque m	park
parquímetro m	parking meter
parte f	part
particular	private
partidas fpl	departures
partir	to break; to leave
a partir de...	from...
Páscoa f	Easter
passadeira f	zebra crossing
passado m	the past
passado(a):	
mal passado(a)	rare (steak)
bem passado(a)	well done (steak)
passageiro(a)	passenger
passagem f	fare; crossing
passagem de nível	level-crossing
passagem de peões	pedestrian crossing
passagem proibida	no right of way
passagem subterrânea m	underpass
passaporte m	passport
passar	to pass; to go by
passatempos mpl	hobbies
passe m	season ticket
passe	go (when crossing road); walk
passear	to go for a walk
passeio m	walk; pavement
pasta f	paste
pasta dentífrica	toothpaste
pastéis mpl	pastries
pastel m	pie; pastry (cake)
pastel folhado	puff pastry
pastelaria f	pastries; café; cake shop
pastilha f	pastille
pastilha elástica	chewing gum
pé m	foot
a pé	on foot
peça f	part; play
peças e acessórios	spares and accessories
pedir	to ask (for)
pedir alguma coisa	to ask for something
pedir emprestado(a)	to borrow
peixe m	fish
pensão m	guesthouse
pensão completa	full board
pensão residencial	boarding house
meia pensão	half board
pensar	to think
pepino m	cucumber
pepino de conserva	gherkin

Portuguese – English

Portuguese – English

pequeno(a)	little; small
pequeno-almoço	breakfast
pêra f	pear
percebes mpl	edible barnacles
perder	to lose; to miss (train, etc)
perdido(a)	lost
perdidos e achados	lost and found; lost property
pergunta f	question
perigo m	danger
perigo de incêndio	fire hazard
perigoso(a)	dangerous
permitir	to allow
perna f	leg
perto (de)	near
peru m	turkey
pesado(a)	heavy
pesar	to weigh
pesca f	fishing

pescada f	hake
pescar	to fish
peso m	weight
pêssego m	peach
pessoa f	person
pessoal adj	personal
pessoal m	staff; personnel
petiscos mpl	snacks; titbits
picada f	sting
picante	spicy
picar	to sting
uma picada de mosquito	a mosquito bite
pilha f	pile; battery (for torch)
pílula f	the pill
pimenta f	pepper
pimento m	pepper (vegetable)
pintar	to paint
pintura f	painting

pior	worse
pisca-pisca m	indicator (on car)
piscina f	swimming pool
piso m	floor; level; surface
piso escorregadio	slippery surface
planta f	plant; map
plateia f	stalls (in theatre)
pneu m	tyre
poder	to be able
poluição f	pollution
polvo m	octopus
pomada f	ointment
pomada para o calçado	shoe polish
ponte f	bridge
população f	population
por	by (through)
por aqui/ por ali	this/that way
por hora	per hour

Portuguese	English
por pessoa	per person
pôr	to put
porção f	portion
porco m	pig; pork
por favor	please
porta f	door
a porta No...	gate number...
portagem f	motorway toll
porteiro m	porter
português m	Portuguese (language)
português (portuguesa)	Portuguese
posologia f	dose (medicine)
postal m	postcard
posto m	post; job
posto clínico	first aid post
posto de socorros	first aid centre
pouco(a)	little
pousada f	state-run hotel; inn

Portuguese	English
povo m	people
praça f	square (in town); market
praça de touros	bullring
praia f	beach; seaside
praticar	to practise
prato m	dish; plate; course of meal
prato da casa	speciality of the house
prato do dia	today's special
prazer m	pleasure
prazer em conhecê-lo	pleased to meet you
precisar de	to need
preciso(a):	
é preciso	it is necessary
preço m	price
preencher	to fill in
prejuízo m	damage
prenda f	gift

Portuguese	English
preocupado(a)	worried
preparado(a)	ready
presente m	gift; present
preservativo m	condom
pressão f	pressure
pressão dos pneus	tyre pressure
preto(a)	black
primavera f	spring (season)
primeiro(a)	first
prioridade f	priority
prioridade à direita	give way to the right
produto m	product; proceeds
produtos alimentares	foodstuffs
professor(a) m/f	teacher
profissão f	profession
profissão, idade, nome	profession, age and name

Portuguese – English

Portuguese – English

Portuguese	English
profundo(a)	deep
proibido(a)	forbidden
proibida a entrada	no entry
proibido estacionar	no parking
proibido fumar	no smoking
proibida a paragem	no stopping
proibida a passagem	no access
proibido pisar a relva	do not walk on the grass
proibido tomar banho	no bathing
promoção *f*	special offer; promotion (at work)
pronto(a)	ready
proprietário(a) *m/f*	owner
provar	to taste; to try on
provisório(a)	temporary
próximo(a) *m*	near; next
público *m*	audience; public
pulmão *m*	lung
puxar	to pull
puxe (sign)	pull (sign)
Q	
quadro *m*	picture; painting
qual	which
quando	when
quanto(a)	how much
quantos(as)?	how many?
quanto tempo? (time)	how long?
quarta-feira *f*	Wednesday
quarto *m*	room; bedroom
quarto de banho	bathroom
quarto com duas camas	twin-bedded room
quarto de casal	double room
quarto individual	single room
que	what
o que é?	what is it?
quebrar	to break
queijada *f*	cheesecake
queijo *m*	cheese
queimadura *f*	burn
queimadura do sol	sunburn *(painful)*
queixa *f*	complaint
quero apresentar uma queixa	I want to make a complaint
quem	who
quente *adj*	hot
querer	to want; to wish
quilo(grama) (kg.) *m*	kilo
quilómetro *m*	kilometre
quinta-feira *f*	Thursday

quiosque *m*	kiosk; newsstand	recolher	to collect
quotidiano(a)	daily	*recolha de bagagem*	baggage
R.		reclaim	
	see **rua**	recompensa *f*	reward
radiografia *f*	X-ray	reconhecer	to recognize
rapariga *f*	girl	recordação *f*	souvenir
rapaz *m*	boy	reembolsar	to reimburse
rápido *m*	express (train)	refeição *f*	meal
rápido(a)	fast	reformado(a)	senior citizen; retired
rato *m*	mouse	*m/f*	
rebuçado *m*	boiled sweet	região *f*	area (region)
recado *m*	message	registar	to register
dar um recado	to give a message	regulamentos *mpl*	regulations
receber	to receive		
receita *f*	recipe	**Reino Unido** *m*	United Kingdom
receita médica	prescription	relógio *m*	watch; clock
recepção *f*	reception	relva *f*	grass
recibo *m*	receipt	*não pisar a relva*	keep off the grass
reclamação *f*	protest; official complaint	remédio *m*	medicine; remedy
reparar	to fix; to repair
---	---
repetir	to repeat
rés-do-chão (R/C) *m*	ground floor
reservar	to book; to reserve
residência *f*	boarding house; residence
responder	to answer; to reply
resposta *f*	answer
reunião *f*	meeting
revista *f*	magazine
rins *mpl*	kidneys
rio *m*	river
rodovia *f*	highway
roteiro *m*	guidebook
roubar	to steal; to rob
roupa *f*	clothes
roupa de cama	bedding
roupa interior	underwear

Portuguese – English

Portuguese – English

rua (R.) f	street	*sala de estar*	living room; lounge	**São (S.)** m	Saint
rubéola f	German measles	*sala de jantar*	dining room	**sapataria** f	shoe shop
ruído m	noise	**salada** f	salad	**sapateira** f	type of crab
		salão m	hall *(for concerts, etc)*	**sapato** m	shoe
S		**salário** m	wage; salary	**sarampo** m	measles
S.	see **São**	**saldo** m	sale	**sardinha** f	sardine
sábado m	Saturday	**salgado(a)**	salty	**satisfeito(a)**	happy; satisfied
saber	to know *(fact)*	**salmão** m	salmon	**saúde** f	health
sabonete m	toilet soap	**salpicão** m	spicy sausage	*saúde!*	cheers!
saco m	bag; handbag	**salsa** f	parsley	*se*	if; whether
saia f	skirt	**salsicha** f	sausage	*se faz favor (SFF)*	please
saídas	departures	**salsicharia** f	delicatessen	**sé** f	cathedral
sair	exit; way out; to go out; to come out	**salteado(a)**	sautéed	**secar**	to dry; to drain *(tank)*
sal m	salt	**sandes** f	sandwich	**seco(a)**	dry
sala f	room	**sanduíche** m	sandwich	**secretária** f	desk
sala de chá	tea room; café	**sangue** m	blood	**secretário(a)** m/f	secretary
sala de embarque	airport lounge	**sanitários** mpl	toilets	**século** m	century
sala de espera	waiting room	**Santo(a) (Sto./Sta.)** m/f	saint	**sede** f	thirst
				ter sede	to be thirsty
				seguir	to follow

Portuguese	English
seguir pela direita	keep to your right
seguir pela esquerda	keep to your left
segunda-feira f	Monday
segundo (time)	second
segundo(a)	second
segundo andar	second floor
de segunda classe	second-class
em segunda mão	second-hand
segurança f	safety
segurar	to hold
seguro m	insurance
seguro contra terceiros	third party insurance
seguro contra todos os riscos	comprehensive insurance
seguro de viagem	travel insurance
seguro(a)	safe; reliable
seio m	breast
selo m	stamp
sem	without
semáforos mpl	traffic lights
semana f	week
para a semana	next week
na semana passada	last week
por semana	weekly (rate, etc)
semanal	weekly
senhor m	sir; gentleman; you
Senhor	Mr
senhora f	lady; madam; you
Senhora	Mrs, Ms
senhorio(a) m/f	landlord/lady
sentar-se	to sit (down)
sentido m	sense; meaning
sentido único	one-way street
sentir	to feel
ser	to be
serviço m	service; cover charge
serviço de quartos	room service
serviço (não) incluído	service (not) included
serviço permanente	24-hour service
servir	to serve
pode servir?	can you serve?
Setembro m	September
seu (sua)	his; her; your
sexta-feira f	Friday
SFF	see **se faz favor**
significar	to mean
sim	yes
simpático(a)	nice; friendly
sinal m	signal; deposit (part payment)
sinal de impedido	engaged tone

Portuguese – English

Portuguese – English

sinal de marcação	dialling tone	
sinal de trânsito	road sign	
sítio m	place; spot	
situado(a)	situated	
só	only; alone	
sobre	over; on top of	
sobre o mar	overlooking the sea	
sobrecarga f	excess load; surcharge	
sobremesa f	dessert	
sócio m	member; partner	
socorro m	help; assistance	
socorro 115	emergency service 999	
socorros e sinistrados	accidents and emergencies	
sogro(a) m/f	father-in-law; mother-in-law	

sol m	sun	
solteiro(a)	single (not married)	
som m	sound	
soma f	amount (sum)	
sopa f	soup	
sorte f	luck; fortune	
boa sorte	good luck	
sorvete m	water ice; sorbet	
sua	see *seu*	
subir	to go up	
suficiente	enough	
sujo(a)	dirty	
sumo m	juice	
supermercado m	supermarket	
surdo(a)	deaf	

T

tabacaria f	tobacconist's; newsagent	
tabaco m	tobacco	

tabela f	list; table	
taberna f	wine bar	
talheres mpl	cutlery	
talho m	butcher's	
talvez	perhaps	
tamanho m	size	
também	also; too	
tamboril m	monkfish	
tanto(a)	so much	
tão	so	
isto é tão bonito	this is so beautiful	
tarde f	afternoon	
boa tarde	good afternoon	
tarde adv	late (in the day)	
tarifa f	charge; rate	
tarifas de portagem	toll charges	
tasca f	tavern; wine bar; restaurant	
taxa f	fee; rate	

taxa de juro	interest rate	
taxa normal	peak-time rate	
taxa reduzida	off-peak rate	
teatro m	theatre	
tele-comandado(a)	remote-controlled	
teleférico m	cable car	
telefonista m/f	operator	
televisão f	television	
tempero m	dressing (for salad); seasoning	
tempestade f	storm	
tempo m	weather; time (duration)	
tempo inteiro	full-time	
tempo parcial	part-time	
temporada f	season	
temporário(a)	temporary	
tensão f	tension	
tensão arterial	high/low blood	

alta/baixa	pressure
tentar	to try
ter	to have
terça-feira f	Tuesday
terceiro(a)	third
para a terceira idade	for the elderly
termas fpl	spa
terra f	earth; ground
terramoto m	earthquake
tesoura f	scissors
tinturaria f	dry-cleaner's
tipo m	sort; kind
tirar	to remove; to take out
tiro m	shot
toalha f	towel
tocar	to touch; to ring; to play
tocar piano	to play the piano
todo(a)	all; the whole

toda a gente	everyone
todas as coisas em toda a parte	everything everywhere
tomar	to take
tomar banho	to bathe; to have a bath
tomar antes de se deitar	take before going to bed
tomar em jejum	take on an empty stomach
tomar ... vezes ao dia	take ... times a day
toranja f	grapefruit
torcer	to twist; to turn
torrada f	toast
torre f	tower
tosse f	cough
tosta f	toasted sandwich

Portuguese - English

Portuguese - English

Portuguese	English
tosta de queijo	toasted cheese sandwich
totoloto m	lottery
toucinho m	bacon
tourada f	bullfight
touro m	bull
trabalhar	to work (person)
trabalho m	work
trabalhos na estrada	roadworks
tradução f	translation
traduzir	to translate
tráfego m	traffic
tranquilo(a)	calm; quiet
transferir	to transfer
trânsito m	traffic
trânsito condicionado	restricted traffic
trânsito proibido	no entry
transtorno m	upset; inconvenience
trás: para trás	backwards
no banco de trás	on the back seat (car)
a parte de trás	the back
tratamento m	treatment
tratar de	to treat; to deal with
travar	to brake
trazer	to bring; to carry
triângulo m	warning triangle
trigo m	wheat
triste	sad
trocar	to exchange; to change
troco m	change (money)
trocos	small change
truta f	trout
tu	you (informal)
tubo m	exhaust pipe; tube; hose
tudo	everything; all

U

Portuguese	English
ultimamente	lately; recently
último(a)	last; latest
ultrapassar	to overtake; to pass
um(a)	a; an; one
único(a)	single; unique
unidade f	unit (hi-fi, etc); unity
unir	to join
usado(a)	used (car, etc)
usar	to use; to wear
útil	useful
utilização f	use
utilizar	to use
uva f	grape

V

Portuguese	English
vaca f	cow
vacina f	vaccination
vagão-restaurante m	buffet car
vagas fpl	vacancies
valer	to be worth
válido(a)	valid
válido(a) até...	valid until...
valor m	value
variado(a)	varied
varicela f	chickenpox
vários(as)	several
vazio(a)	empty
velho(a)	old
velocidade f	gear; speed
velocidade limitada	speed limit in force
vencimento m	wage; expiry date
venda f	sale (in general)
venda proibida	not for public sale
vendas e reparações	sales and repairs
vender	to sell
vende-se	for sale
vento m	wind
ver	to see; to look at
verão m	summer
verdade f	truth
não é verdade?	isn't it?
verdadeiro(a)	true
verde	green
verificar	to check
vermelho(a)	red
véspera f	the day before; the eve
vestiário m	cloakroom; changing room
vestido m	dress
vestir	to dress; to wear
vestir-se	to get dressed
veterinário(a) m/f	vet
vez f	time; turn
às vezes	occasionally; sometimes
uma vez	once
duas vezes	twice
muitas vezes	often
é a sua vez	it's your turn
via f	via, lane
via aérea	by air mail
via nasal	to be inhaled
via oral	orally
viaduto m	viaduct; flyover
viagem f	trip; journey
viagem de negócios	business trip
viajar	to travel
vida f	life
vidros mpl	glassware

Portuguese – English

Portuguese – English

vila *f*	small town
vindima *f*	harvest (of grapes)
vinho *m*	wine
vir	to come
virar	to turn
vire à direita	turn right
vire à esquerda	turn left
visitar	to visit
vista *f*	view
com linda	with a beautiful
vista	view
visto *m*	visa
vitela *f*	veal
vivenda *f*	chalet; villa
viver	to live
vivo(a)	alive
vizinho(a) *m/f*	neighbour
você(s)	you

volta *f*	turn
à volta (de)	about
em volta (de)	around
dar uma volta	to go for a short walk/ride
voltar	to return
	(go/come back)
volto já	I'll be back in a minute
voo *m*	flight
voo fretado	charter flight
voo normal	scheduled flight
vos	you; to you
vós	you
vosso	yours

W

wind-surf *m*	windsurfing

X

xadrez *m*	chess
xarope *m*	syrup
xarope para a tosse	cough syrup
xerez *m*	sherry

Z

zona *f*	zone
zona azul	permitted parking zone
zona de banhos	swimming area
zona interdita	no thoroughfare

Further titles in Collins' phrasebook range
Collins Gem Phrasebook

Also available as Phrasebook CD Pack
Other titles in the series

Arabic	Greek	Polish
Cantonese	Italian	Portuguese
Croatian	Japanese	Russian
Czech	Korean	Spanish
Dutch	Latin American	Thai
French	Spanish	Turkish
German	Mandarin	Vietnamese

Collins Phrasebook & Dictionary

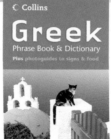

Also available as **Phrasebook CD Pack**

Other titles in the series

German Japanese Portuguese Spanish

Collins Easy: Photo Phrasebook

Also available as

Phrasebook CD Pack

Other titles in the series
Easy French
Easy Greek
Easy Italian

To order any of these titles, please telephone 0870 787 1732. For further information about all Collins books, visit our website: www.collins.co.uk